The Canadian's Guide to Accounting

by John A. Tracy, CPA, and
Cécile Laurin, CPA, CA

WILEY

Publisher's Acknowledgments

Authors: John A. Tracy, CPA, and Cécile Laurin, CPA, CA

Senior Acquisitions Editor: Tracy Boggier

Project Manager: Susan Pink

Compilation Editor: Georgette Beatty

Production Editor: Magesh Elangovan

Cover Design: Wiley

Cover Images: © Bakai/Getty Images, © stockish/Shutterstock

The Canadian's Guide to Accounting

Published by John Wiley & Sons, Inc.
111 River St.
Hoboken, NJ 07030-5774
http://www.wiley.com

For general information on our other products and services, please contact our Business Development Department in the U.S. at 317-572-3205.

Library of Congress Control Number: 2019942830

ISBN 978-1-119-60934-6 (pbk)

Manufactured in the United States of America

V10011106_061319

Table of Contents

1

Financial Statements and Accounting Standards

The three primary business financial statements are the income statement, the balance sheet, and the statement of cash flows. In this chapter, you get some juicy details.

For each financial statement, this chapter introduces its basic information components. The purpose of financial statements is to communicate information that is useful to the readers of the financial statements, to those who are entitled to the information. Financial statement readers include the managers of the business and its lenders and investors. These constitute the primary audience for financial statements.

 Think of yourself as a shareholder in a business. What sort of information would you want to know about the business? The answer to this question should be the touchstone for the accountant in preparing the financial statements.

This chapter also briefly discusses financial accounting and reporting standards. Businesses comply with established rules for recording revenue, gains, expenses, and losses; for putting values on assets and liabilities; and for presenting and disclosing information in their financial reports. The basic idea is that all businesses should follow uniform methods for measuring and reporting profit performance, and reporting financial condition and cash flows. Consistency in accounting from business to business is the goal. This chapter explains who makes the rules and discusses two important developments: the internationalization of accounting standards, and the increasing divide between financial reporting for public and private companies.

The Information Content of Financial Statements

This chapter focuses on the basic *information components* of each financial statement reported by a business. The first step is to get a good idea of the information content reported in financial statements. The second step is to become familiar with the architecture, rules of classification, and other features of financial statements.

An introduction to the business example

To better illustrate the three primary financial statements, this chapter uses a realistic business example. The information content of its financial statements depends on the line of business a company is in — in other words, which types of products and services it sells. The financial statements of a movie theatre chain are different from those of a bank, which are different from those of an airline, which are different from an automobile manufacturer. This chapter uses a fairly common type of business example.

Here are the particulars of the business for the example:

- It sells products, mainly to other businesses.
- It sells on credit, and its customers take a month or so before they pay.
- It holds a fairly large stock of products awaiting sale (its inventory).
- It owns a wide variety of long-term operating assets that have useful lives from 2 to 30 years or longer (a building, machines, tools, computers, office furniture, and so on).
- It's been in business for many years and has made a steady profit over the years.
- It borrows money for part of the total capital it needs.

- It's organized as a corporation and pays federal and provincial income taxes on its annual taxable income.
- It has never been in bankruptcy and is not facing any immediate financial difficulties.

Upcoming figures present the company's annual income statement for the year just ended, its balance sheet at the end of the year, and its statement of cash flows for the year. Dollar amounts in the three financials are rounded off to the nearest thousand, which is not uncommon. Dollar amounts can be reported out to the last dollar, or even the last penny for that matter. But too many digits in a dollar amount are hard to absorb, so many businesses round off the dollar amounts in their financial statements.

These financial statements are stepping-stone illustrations that are concerned mainly with the basic information components in each statement. The financial statements in this chapter do not include all the information you see in actual financial statements. Also, descriptive labels are used for each item rather than the terse and technical titles you see in actual financial statements. And subtotals that you see in actual financial statements are stripped out because they are not necessary at this point. So, with all these conventions in mind, let's get going.

Financial statements are characteristically stiff and formal. No slang or street language is allowed. Seldom do you see any graphics or artwork in a financial statement itself, although you do see a fair number of photos and graphics elsewhere in the annual reports of public companies. And virtually no humour appears in financial reports. (However, in his annual letter to the shareholders of Berkshire Hathaway, Warren Buffett includes some wonderful humour to make his points.)

The income statement

The *income statement* is the all-important financial statement that summarizes the profit-making activities of a business over a period of time. Its more formal name is the *statement of financial performance.* Figure 1-1 shows the basic information content for an external income statement: one released outside the business to its owners and lenders.

Company's Name
Income Statement
for Most Recent Year
(Dollar amounts in thousands)

Sales revenue	$10,400
Cost of goods sold expense	6,240
Selling, general, and administrative expenses	3,235
Interest expense	125
Income tax expense	280
Net income	$520

Figure 1-1: *Basic information components of the income statement*

The income statement in Figure 1-1 shows six lines of information: sales revenue on the top line, four types of expenses that are deducted from sales revenue, and finally, bottom-line net income. Virtually all income statements disclose at least the four expenses shown in Figure 1-1. The first two expenses (cost of goods sold and selling, general, and administrative expenses) take a big bite out of sales revenue. The other two expenses (interest and income tax) are relatively small as a percentage of annual sales revenue but important enough in their own right to be reported separately.

Instead of one amount for all selling, general, and administrative expenses, a business may separate out certain expenses from this broad category. For example, a business could disclose separate expenses for advertising and sales promotion, depreciation, salaries and wages, research and development, and delivery and shipping — though reporting these expenses is not common. Businesses do not disclose the compensation of top management in their external financial reports.

Inside most businesses, an income statement is called a *P&L (profit and loss) report*. These internal profit performance reports to the managers of a business include a good deal more detailed information about expenses as well as about sales revenue. Reporting just four expenses to managers (as shown in Figure 1-1) would not do.

Sales revenue is from the sales of products and services to customers. *Other revenues and gains* refer to amounts earned by a business from sources other than sales: for example, a real estate rental business receives rental income from its tenants. (In the example, the business has only sales revenue.) As mentioned, businesses report the expenses shown in Figure 1-1 — cost of goods sold expense, selling and general expenses, interest expense, and income tax expense. Further breakdown of expenses is at the business's discretion.

Net income, being the bottom line of the income statement after deducting all expenses from sales revenue (and gains, if any), is called, not surprisingly, the *bottom line.* It is also called *net earnings.* A few companies call it *profit* or *net profit.*

The income statement gets the most attention from business managers, lenders, and investors (not that they ignore the other two financial statements). The much abbreviated versions of income statements that you see in the financial press or on financial Internet sites report the top line (sales revenue), the bottom line (net income), and not much more. Refer to Chapter 3 for much more information on income statements.

The balance sheet

Figure 1-2 shows the basic information components of a typical balance sheet. One reason the balance sheet is called by this name is that its two sides balance, or are equal in total amounts.

In the example, the $5.2 million total of assets equals the $5.2 million total of liabilities and owners' equity. The balance, or equality, of total assets on the one hand and the sum of liabilities plus owners' equity on the other hand is expressed in the accounting equation.

Company's Name
Balance Sheet
at End of Most Recent Year
(Dollar amounts in thousands)

Assets	
Cash	$1,000
Receivables from sales made on credit	800
Inventory of unsold products, at cost	1,560
Long-term operating assets, at cost less cumulative amount charged off to depreciation expense	1,840
Total assets	$5,200

Liabilities and Owners' Equity	
Non-interest-bearing liabilities from purchases on credit and for unpaid expenses	$650
Interest-bearing debt	2,080
Owners' equity capital invested in business plus profit earned and retained in business	2,470
Total liabilities and owners' equity	$5,200

Figure 1-2: *Basic information components of the balance sheet*

In general, five or more assets are reported in a typical balance sheet, starting with cash, and then receivables, and then cost of products held for sale, and so on down the line. Generally five or more liabilities are disclosed, starting with trade credit liabilities (from buying on credit), then unpaid expenses, and then proceeding through the interest-bearing debts of the business. Two or more owners' equity accounts are generally reported. In summary, you'll find 12 or more lines of information in most balance sheets. Each of these information packets is called an *account* — so a balance sheet has a composite of asset accounts, liability accounts, and owners' equity accounts.

Most businesses need a variety of assets. You have *cash*, which every business needs, of course. Businesses that sell products carry an *inventory* of products awaiting sale to customers. Businesses need long-term resources that are generally called *property, plant, and equipment*; this group includes buildings, vehicles, tools, machines, and other resources needed in their operations. All these and more go under the collective name *assets*.

As you'd suspect, the particular assets reported in the balance sheet depend on which assets the business owns. Just four basic assets are included in Figure 1-2. These are the hardcore assets that a business selling products on credit would have. In this example, the business owns *fixed assets*. They are *fixed* because they are held for use in the business's operations and are not for sale, and their usefulness lasts several years or longer.

So, where does a business get the money to buy its assets? Most businesses borrow money on the basis of interest-bearing bank loans, promissory notes, or other credit instruments for part of the total capital they need for their assets. Also, businesses buy many things on credit and at the balance sheet date owe money to their suppliers, which will be paid in the future. These operating liabilities are never grouped with interest-bearing debt in the balance sheet. The accountant would be tied to the stake for doing such a thing.

Note that liabilities are not intermingled among assets — this is a definite no-no in financial reporting. You cannot subtract certain liabilities from certain assets and report only the net balance.

Could a business's total liabilities be greater than its total assets? Well, not likely — unless the business has been losing money hand over fist. In the vast majority of cases, a business has more total assets than total liabilities. Why? For two reasons:

- Its owners have invested money in the business, which is not a liability of the business.

- The business has earned profit over the years, and some (or all) of the profit has been retained in the business. Making profit increases assets; if not all the profit is distributed to owners, the company's assets increase by the amount of profit retained.

In the example (refer to Figure 1-2), owners' equity is about $2.5 million, $2.47 million to be exact. Sometimes this amount is referred to as *net worth* because it equals total assets minus total liabilities. However, net worth is not a good term because it implies that the business is worth the amount recorded in its owners' equity accounts. The market value of a business, when it needs to be known, depends on many factors. The amount of owners' equity reported in a balance sheet, which is called its *book value,* is not irrelevant in setting a market value on the business but is usually not the dominant factor. The amount of owners' equity in a balance sheet is based on the history of capital invested in the business by its owners and the history of its profit performance and distributions from profit.

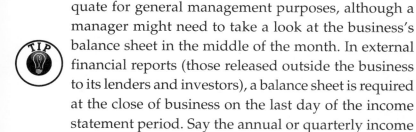

A balance sheet could be whipped up anytime you want — say, at the end of every day. Typically, preparing a balance sheet at the end of each month is adequate for general management purposes, although a manager might need to take a look at the business's balance sheet in the middle of the month. In external financial reports (those released outside the business to its lenders and investors), a balance sheet is required at the close of business on the last day of the income statement period. Say the annual or quarterly income statement ends September 30; the business would reports its balance sheet at the close of business on September 30.

The balance sheet could more properly be called the *statement of assets, liabilities, and owners' equity.* Its more formal name is the *statement of financial position.* Just a reminder: The profit *for the most recent period* is found in the income statement; periodic profit is not reported in the balance sheet. The profit reported in the income statement is before any distributions from profit to owners. The cumulative amount of profit over the years that has not been distributed to its owners is reported in the owners' equity section of the company's balance sheet.

 By the way, note that the balance sheet in Figure 1-2 is presented in two formats:

- Report format is a top and bottom format (also called portrait mode).
- Account format is a left and right side format (also called landscape mode).

Either format is acceptable.

The statement of cash flows

To survive and thrive, business managers fulfill three financial imperatives:

- Make an adequate profit
- Keep the financial condition out of trouble and in good shape
- Control cash flows

The income statement reports whether the business made a profit. The balance sheet reports the business's financial condition. The third imperative is reported on in the *statement of cash flows*, which presents a summary of the business's sources and uses of cash during the income statement period.

Smart business managers hardly get the words *net income* (or profit) out of their mouths before mentioning *cash flow*. Successful business managers tell you that they have to manage both profit *and* cash flow; you can't do one and ignore the other. Business is a two-headed dragon in this respect. Ignoring cash flow can pull the rug out from under a successful profit formula. Still, some managers are preoccupied with making profit and overlook cash flow.

For external financial reporting, the cash flows of a business are divided into three categories, which are shown in Figure 1-3.

In the example, the company earned $520,000 profit during the year (see Figure 1-1). One result of its profit-making activities was an increase of $400,000 in cash, which you see in part 1 of the statement of cash flows (see Figure 1-3). This still leaves $120,000 of profit to explain (see the next section). The actual cash inflows from revenues and outflows for expenses run on a different timetable than the recording of the sales revenue and expenses for determining profit. It's like two different trains going to the same destination — the second train (the cash flow train) runs on a different schedule than the first train (the recording of sales revenue and expenses in the business's accounts).

Company's Name
Statement of Cash Flows
for Most Recent Year
(Dollar amounts in thousands)

(1) Cash effect during period from operating activities (collecting cash from sales and paying cash for expenses)	$400
(2) Cash effect during period from making investments in long-term operating assets	(450)
(3) Cash effect during period from dealings with lenders and owners	200
Cash increase during period	150
Cash at start of year	850
Cash at end of year	$1,000

Figure 1-3: *Basic information components in the statement of cash flows*

The next section presents a scenario that accounts for the $120,000 difference between cash flow and profit. For a more comprehensive explanation of the differences between cash flows and sales revenue and expenses, see Chapter 5.

The second part of the statement of cash flows sums the long-term investments made by the business during the year, such as constructing a new production plant or replacing machinery and equipment. If the business sold any of its long-term assets, it reports the cash inflows from these disposals in this section of the statement of cash flows. The cash flows of other investment activities (if any) are reported in this part of the statement as well. As you can see in part 2 of the statement of cash flows (see Figure 1-3), the business invested $450,000 in new long-term operating assets (trucks, equipment, tools, and computers).

The third part of the statement sums the dealings between the business and its sources of capital during the period — borrowing money from lenders and raising new capital from its owners. Cash outflows to pay debt are reported in this section, as well as cash distributions from profit paid to the business's owners. As you can see in part 3 of the statement of cash flows (see Figure 1-3), the result of these transactions was to increase cash by $200,000. Note that in this example, the business did not make cash distributions from profit to its owners. It could have, but it didn't — which is an important point (see the later section "Why no cash distribution from profit?").

As you see in Figure 1-3, the net result of the three types of cash activities was a $150,000 increase during the year. The increase is added to the cash balance at the start of the year to get the cash balance at the end of the year, which is $1 million. Note that the $150,000 increase in cash during the year (in this example) is never referred to as a cash flow *bottom line*, or any such thing. The term *bottom line* is strictly reserved for the last line of the income statement, which reports net income — the final profit after all expenses are deducted.

The statements of cash flows reported by most businesses are frustratingly difficult to read. (Find out more about this issue in Chapter 5.) Figure 1-3 presents the statement of cash flows for the business example as simply as possible. Actual cash flow statements are much more complicated than the brief introduction to this financial statement that you see in Figure 1-3.

Imagine you have a highlighter in your hand, and the three basic financial statements of a business are in front of you. What are the most important numbers to mark? Financial statements do not come with headlines, like newspapers. You have to find your own headlines. Bottom-line profit (net income) in the income statement is one number you should mark. Another key number is *cash flow from operating activities* in the statement of cash flows.

How Profit and Cash Flow from Profit Differ

The income statement in Figure 1-1 reports that the business in the example earned $520,000 in net income for the year. However, the statement of cash flows in Figure 1-3 reports that its profit-making, or operating, activities increased cash only

$400,000 during the year. This gap between profit and cash flow from operating activities is not unusual.

So, what happened to the other $120,000 of profit? Is some accounting sleight of hand going on? Did the business really earn $520,000 net income if cash increased only $400,000? These are good questions, and this section tries to answer them as directly as possible without hitting you over the head with a lot of technical details.

Here's one scenario that explains the $120,000 difference between profit (net income) and cash flow from operating activities:

- Suppose the business collected $50,000 less cash from customers during the year than the total sales revenue reported in its income statement. (Note that the business sells on credit and its customers take time before paying the business.) Therefore, a cash flow lag happens between booking sales and collecting cash from customers. As a result, the business's cash inflow from customers was $50,000 less than the sales revenue amount used to calculate profit for the year.

- Also suppose that during the year the business made cash payments connected with its expenses that were $70,000 higher than the total amount of expenses reported in the income statement. For example, a business that sells products buys or makes the products, and then holds the products in inventory for some time before it sells the items to customers. Cash is paid out before the cost of goods sold expense is recorded. This is one example of a difference between cash flow connected with an expense and the amount recorded in the income statement for the expense.

In this scenario, the two factors cause cash flow from profit-making (operating) activities to be $120,000 less than the net income earned for the year. Cash collections from customers were $50,000 less than sales revenue, and cash payments for expenses were $70,000 more than the amount of expenses recorded to the year. Chapter 5 explains the several factors that cause cash flow and bottom-line profit to diverge.

At this point the key idea to hold in mind is that the sales revenue reported in the income statement does not equal cash collections from customers during the year, and expenses do not equal cash payments during the year. Cash collections from sales minus cash payments for expenses gives cash flow from a company's profit-making activities; sales revenue minus expenses gives the net income earned for the year. Cash flow almost always is different from net income.

Key Information from Financial Statements

The point of reporting financial statements is to provide important information to people who have a financial interest in the business — mainly its outside investors and lenders. From that information, investors and lenders can answer key questions about the business's financial performance and condition. This section discusses some of these key questions.

How's profit performance?

Investors use two important measures to judge a company's annual profit performance. Here is the data from Figures 1-1 and 1-2 (the dollar amounts are in thousands):

- **Return on sales** = profit as a percentage of annual sales revenue:

  $520 bottom-line annual profit (net income) ÷ $10,400 annual sales revenue = 5.0%

- **Return on equity** = profit as a percentage of owners' equity:

  $520 bottom-line annual profit (net income) ÷ $2,470 owners' equity = 21.1%

Profit looks pretty thin compared with annual sales revenue. The company earns only 5 percent return on sales. In other words, 95 cents out of every sales dollar goes for expenses, and the company keeps only 5 cents for profit. (Many businesses earn 10 percent or higher return on sales.) However, when profit is compared with owners' equity, things look a lot better. The business earns more than 21 percent profit on its owners' equity. You probably don't have many investments earning 21 percent per year.

Is there enough cash?

Cash is the lubricant of business activity. Realistically, a business can't operate with a zero cash balance. It can't wait to open the morning mail or look at the bank account online to see how much cash it will have for the day's needs (although some businesses try to operate on a shoestring cash balance). A business should keep enough cash on hand to keep things running smoothly even when interruptions occur in the normal inflows of cash. A business has to meet its payroll on time, for example. Keeping an adequate balance in the chequing account serves as a buffer against unforeseen disruptions in normal cash inflows.

At the end of the year, the business in the example has $1 million cash on hand (refer to Figure 1-2). This cash balance is available for general business purposes. (If restrictions exist on how it can use its cash balance, the business is obligated to disclose those restrictions.) Is $1 million enough? Interestingly, businesses do not have to comment on their cash balance.

The business has $650,000 in operating liabilities that will come due for payment over the next month or so (refer to Figure 1-2). So, it has enough cash to pay these liabilities. But it doesn't have enough cash on hand to pay its operating liabilities and its $2.08 million interest-bearing debt (refer to Figure 1-2). Lenders don't expect a business to keep a cash balance more than the amount of debt; this condition would defeat the purpose of lending money to the business, which is to have the business put the money to good use and be able to pay interest on the debt.

Lenders are more interested in the business's capability to control its cash flows so that when the time comes to pay off loans it will be able to do so. They know that the business's other, non-cash assets will be converted into cash flow. Receivables will be collected, and products held in inventory will be sold and the sales will generate cash flow. So, you shouldn't focus just on cash; throw the net wider and look at the other assets as well.

Taking this broader approach, the business has $1 million cash, $800,000 receivables, and $1.56 million inventory, which adds up to $3.36 million of cash and cash potential. Relative to its $2.73 million total liabilities ($650,000 operating liabilities plus $2.08 million debt), the business looks in pretty good shape. On the other hand, if it turns out that the business is not able to collect its receivables and is not able to sell its products, it would end up in deep trouble.

One other way to look at a business's cash balance is to express its cash balance in terms of how many days of sales the amount represents. In the example, the business has an ending cash balance equal to 35 days of sales, calculated as follows:

- $10,400,000 annual sales revenue ÷ 365 days = $28,493 sales per day
- $1,000,000 cash balance ÷ $28,493 sales per day = 35 days

The business's cash balance equals a little more than one month of sales activity, which most lenders and investors would consider adequate.

Can you trust the financial statement numbers?

Whether the financial statements are correct or not depends on the answers to two basic questions:

- Does the business have a reliable accounting system in place and employ competent accountants?

- Has top management manipulated the business's accounting methods or deliberately falsified the numbers?

Many businesses don't put much effort into keeping their accounting systems up to speed, and they skimp on hiring competent accountants. In short, a risk exists that the financial statements of a business could be incorrect and seriously misleading.

To increase the credibility of their financial statements, many businesses hire independent auditors to examine their accounting systems and records and to express opinions on whether the financial statements present fairly the reality of the company's performance and conditions and the preparation of the statement conforms to established accounting standards. In fact, some business lenders insist on an annual audit by an independent public accounting firm as a condition of making the loan. The outside, non-management investors in a privately owned business could vote to have annual audits of the financial statements. Public companies have no choice; a public company is required to have annual audits by an independent public accounting firm.

Two points: Audits are not cheap, and these audits are not always effective in rooting out financial reporting fraud by high-level managers.

Why no cash distribution from profit?

In this chapter's example, the business did not distribute any of its profit for the year to its owners. Distributions from profit by a business corporation are called *dividends*. (The total amount distributed is divided up among the shareholders, hence the term *dividends*.) Cash distributions from profit to owners are included in the third section of the statement of cash flows (refer to Figure 1-3). But in the example, the business did not make any cash distributions from profit — even though it earned $520,000 net income (refer to Figure 1-1). Why not?

The business realized $400,000 cash flow from its profit-making (operating) activities (refer to Figure 1-3). In most cases, this would be the upper limit on how much cash a business would distribute from profit to its owners. So you might very well ask whether the business should have distributed, say, at least half of its cash flow from profit, or $200,000, to its owners. If you owned 20 percent of the business's ownership shares, you would have received 20 percent, or $40,000, of the distribution. But you got no cash return on your investment in the business. Your shares should be worth more because the profit for the year increased the company's owners' equity. But you did not see any of this increase in your wallet.

Deciding whether to make cash distributions from profit to shareholders is in the hands of the directors of a business corporation. Its shareowners elect the directors, and in theory the directors act in the best interests of the shareholders. Evidently the directors thought the business had better uses for the $400,000 cash flow from profit than distributing some of it to shareholders.

Generally, the main reason for not making cash distributions from profit is to finance the business's growth — to use all the cash flow from profit for expanding the assets needed by the business at the higher sales level. Ideally, the business's directors would explain their decision not to distribute any money from profit to the shareholders. But, generally, no such comments are made in financial reports.

In Step with Accounting and Financial Reporting Standards

The unimpeded flow of capital is critical in a free-market economic system and in the international flow of capital between countries. Investors and lenders put their capital to work where they think they can get the best returns on their investments consistent with the risks they're willing to take. To make these decisions, they need the accounting information provided in financial statements of businesses.

Imagine the confusion that would result if every business were permitted to invent its own accounting methods for measuring profit and for putting values on assets and liabilities. What if every business adopted its own individual accounting terminology and followed its own style for presenting financial statements? Such a state of affairs would be a Tower of Babel.

Canadian and international standards

The authoritative standards and rules that govern financial accounting and reporting by businesses based in Canada are called *generally accepted accounting principles* (GAAP). When you read the financial statements of a business, you're entitled to assume that the business has fully complied with GAAP in reporting its cash flows, profit-making activities, and financial condition — unless the business makes clear that it has prepared its financial statements using some other basis of accounting or has deviated from GAAP in one or more significant respects.

If a business does not use GAAP as the basis for preparing its financial statements, the business should make clear which other basis of accounting is being used and should avoid using financial statement titles that are associated with GAAP. For example, if a business such as a farm uses a simple cash receipts and cash disbursements basis of accounting — which falls

way short of GAAP — it should not use the terms *income statement* and *balance sheet*. These terms are part and parcel of GAAP, and their use as titles for financial statements implies that the business is using GAAP.

The general consensus (backed up by law) is that businesses should use consistent accounting methods and terminology. Bombardier and BCE should use the same accounting methods; so should BlackBerry and Canadian Tire. Of course, businesses in different industries have different types of transactions, but the same types of transactions should be accounted for in the same way. That is the goal.

Around 4,000 publicly owned corporations have their shares traded on the Toronto Stock Exchange (TSX). All businesses *should* use the same rulebook of GAAP. However, the rulebook permits alternative accounting methods for some transactions. Furthermore, accountants have to interpret the rules as they apply GAAP in actual situations. The devil is in the details.

In Canada, as in the majority of countries around the globe, GAAP, which includes international standards, constitutes the gold standard for preparing financial statements of business entities. The presumption is that any deviations from GAAP would cause misleading financial statements. If a business honestly thinks it should deviate from GAAP — to better reflect the economic reality of its transactions or situation — it should make clear that it has not complied with GAAP in one or more respects. If the business does not disclose the deviations from GAAP, the business may have legal exposure to those who relied on the information in its financial report and suffered a loss attributable to the misleading nature of the information.

Canadian, U.S., and international standard setters

Okay, so everyone reading a financial report is entitled to assume that GAAP has been followed — unless the business clearly discloses that it is using another basis of accounting.

The basic idea behind the development of GAAP is to measure profit and to value assets and liabilities *consistently* from business to business — to establish broad-scale uniformity in accounting methods for all businesses. The idea is to make sure that all accountants are singing the same tune from the same hymnal. The purpose is also to establish realistic and objective methods for measuring profit and putting values on assets and liabilities. The authoritative bodies write the tunes that accountants have to sing.

Who are these authoritative bodies? Canada has two bodies setting standards for businesses:

- The main authoritative accounting standards setter is the International Accounting Standards Board (IASB), which is based in London. The standards set by this body are called International Financial Reporting Standards (IFRS) and they have been adopted by Canada for all publicly traded companies. These standards can be found in Part I of the *CPA Canada Handbook.*

- The second body making pronouncements on Canadian GAAP for private enterprises and for keeping these accounting standards up-to-date is the Accounting Standards Board (AcSB) of CPA Canada. The standards set by this body are called Accounting Standards for Private Enterprises (ASPE) and can be found in Part II of the *CPA Canada Handbook.*

The body in the United States is the Financial Accounting Standards Board (FASB). Unlike in Canada, the U.S. federal Securities and Exchange Commission (SEC) has broad powers over accounting and financial reporting standards for publicly traded companies.

All GAAP (Canadian, U.S., and international) also include minimum requirements for *disclosure*, which refers to how information is classified and presented in financial statements and to the types of information that have to be included with the financial statements, mainly as notes.

Some people think the rules have become too complicated and far too technical. If you flip through the many parts of the *Handbook*, you'll see why people come to this conclusion. However, if the rules are not specific and detailed enough, different accountants will make different interpretations that will cause inconsistency from one business to the next regarding how profit is measured and how assets and liabilities are reported in the balance sheet. The AcSB was between a rock and a hard place. Consequently, two sets of GAAP were put into place — one for public companies (IFRS) and one for private companies (ASPE). For the most part the AcSB issues rules that are detailed and technical but take care of the major concerns of most businesses.

Worldwide accounting

Although it's a bit of an overstatement, today the investment of capital knows no borders. Canadian capital is invested in European and other countries, and capital from other countries is invested in Canadian businesses. In short, the flow of capital has become international. Recognizing the need, the AcSB joined the IASB and adopted IFRS for public companies.

The need to make GAAP uniform globally (at least for public companies) also applies to the United States. Of course, political issues and national pride come into play in trying to achieve this goal. The term *harmonization* is favoured, which sidesteps difficult issues regarding the future roles of the FASB and IASB in the issuance of international accounting standards.

One major obstacle deterring the goal of worldwide accounting standards concerns which sort of standards should be issued:

- The FASB follows a *rules-based* approach. Its pronouncements have been detailed and technical. The idea is to leave little room for differences of interpretation.

- The IASB favours a *principles-based* method. Under this approach, accounting standards are stated in fairly broad general language and the detailed interpretation of the standards is left to accountants in the field.

The two authoritative bodies have disagreed on some key accounting issues, and the road to convergence of accounting standards may be rocky.

In Canada and internationally, the guidelines are more flexible. Accountants use their professional judgment and experience to decide which method is best in situations where different options for how to account for transactions are available. Accountants use additional sources of GAAP outside the *Handbook* to decide which accounting practice to follow.

No country's economy is an island to itself. The stability, development, and growth of an economy depend on securing capital from both inside and outside the country. The flow of capital across borders by investors and lenders gives enormous impetus for the development of uniform international accounting standards. Stay tuned; in the coming years, you may see more and more convergence of accounting standards in the remaining countries that have not yet adopted IFRS.

A divide between public and private companies

Up until the adoption of IFRS for public companies, GAAP and financial reporting standards were viewed as equally applicable to public companies (generally large corporations) and private (generally smaller) companies. There was a growing distinction between accounting and financial reporting standards for public versus private companies. Although most accountants don't like to admit it, there has always been a de facto divergence in financial reporting practices by private companies compared with the more rigorously enforced standards for public companies.

It's probably safe to say that the financial reports of most private businesses measure up to GAAP standards in all significant respects. At the same time, however, little doubt exists that the financial reports of some private companies fall short. Private companies do not have many of the accounting problems of large, public companies. For example, many public companies deal in complex derivative instruments, issue stock options to managers, provide highly developed defined-benefit retirement and health benefit plans for their employees, enter into complicated inter-company investment and joint venture operations, have complex organizational structures, and so on. Most private companies do not have to deal with these issues.

Finally, smaller private businesses do not have as much money to spend on their accountants and auditors. Big companies can spend big bucks and hire highly qualified accountants. Furthermore, public companies are legally required to have annual audits by independent public accountants. The annual audit keeps a big business up-to-date on accounting and financial reporting standards. Frankly, smaller private companies are at a disadvantage in keeping up with accounting and financial reporting standards.

How income tax methods influence accounting methods

Generally speaking, the income tax accounting rules for determining the annual taxable income of a business are in agreement with GAAP. In other words, the accounting methods used for figuring taxable income and for figuring business profit before income tax are in general agreement. But several differences do exist. A business may use one accounting method for filing its annual income tax returns and a different method for measuring its annual profit both internally for management reporting and externally for preparing its financial statements to outsiders.

Many people argue that certain income tax accounting methods have had an unhealthy effect on GAAP. If a particular accounting method is allowed for determining annual taxable income, the path of least resistance is for a business to use the same method for preparing its financial statements. For example, the income tax laws permit accelerated methods for depreciating long-lived operating assets — software, computers, tools, and autos and trucks. (Even the cost of buildings can be depreciated over shorter life spans than the actual lives of most buildings.) Other depreciation methods might be more realistic, but many businesses use accelerated depreciation methods both in their income tax returns and in their financial statements.

Interpretation of the rules

An often repeated accounting story concerns three people interviewing for an important accounting position. They are asked one key question: "What's 2 plus 2?" The first candidate answers, "It's 4," and is told, "Don't call us, we'll call you." The second candidate answers, "Well, most of the time the answer is 4, but sometimes it's 3 and sometimes it's 5." The third candidate answers: "What do you want the answer to be?" Guess who gets the job. This story exaggerates, of course, but it does have an element of truth.

> The point is that interpreting GAAP is not cut and dried. Many accounting standards leave a lot of wiggle room for interpretation. *Guidelines* would be a better word to describe many accounting rules. Deciding how to account for certain transactions and situations requires seasoned judgment and careful analysis of the rules. Furthermore, many estimates have to be made. Deciding on accounting methods requires, above all else, good faith.

A business might resort to creative accounting to make profit for the period look better, or to make its year-to-year profit less erratic than it really is (which is called *income smoothing*). Like lawyers who know where to find loopholes, accountants can come up with inventive interpretations that stay within the boundaries of GAAP. Massaging the numbers can get out of hand and become accounting fraud, also called cooking the books. Massaging the numbers has some basis in honest differences for interpreting the facts. Cooking the books goes way beyond interpreting facts; this fraud consists of *inventing* facts and good old-fashioned chicanery.

2

Bookkeeping and Accounting Systems

It's safe to say that most folks are not enthusiastic bookkeepers. You may balance your chequebook against your bank statement or your online bank activity report every month or so and somehow manage to pull together all information you need for your annual income tax return. But if you're like a lot of folks, you use the paperless feature with most of the businesses you deal with, use the automatic debit feature offered by your bank, pay most bills with your credit card, and stuff your other bills in a drawer and just drag them out once or twice a month to pay them. You may have been caught not paying a bill on time because of all the automated payment options at your disposal.

And when was the last time you prepared a detailed listing of all your assets and liabilities (even though a listing of assets is a good idea for fire insurance purposes)? Personal computer programs and phone apps are available to make bookkeeping for individuals more organized, but you still have to enter a lot of data into the program, and most people decide not to put forth the effort.

Individuals can get along quite well without much bookkeeping — but the opposite is true for a business. One key difference exists between individuals and businesses. Every business must prepare periodic financial statements, the accuracy of which is critical to the business's survival. The business depends on the accounts and records that its bookkeeping process generates to prepare these statements; if the accounting records are incomplete or inaccurate, the financial statements are incomplete or inaccurate. And inaccuracy simply won't do. In fact, inaccurate and incomplete bookkeeping records could be construed as evidence of incompetence or fraud.

Obviously, then, business managers have to be sure that the company's bookkeeping and accounting system is adequate and reliable. This chapter shows you what bookkeepers and accountants do, mainly so you have a clear idea of what it takes to be sure that the information coming out of your accounting system is complete, timely, and accurate.

Bookkeeping and Beyond

Bookkeeping refers mainly to the recordkeeping aspects of accounting; it is essentially the process (some would say the drudgery) of recording all the information regarding the transactions and financial activities of a business (or other organization, venture, or project). Bookkeeping is an indispensable subset of accounting.

The term *accounting* is much broader, going into the realm of designing the bookkeeping system, establishing controls to make sure the system is working well, and analyzing and verifying the recorded information. Accountants give orders; bookkeepers follow them.

Think of accounting as what goes on before and after bookkeeping. Accountants prepare reports based on the information accumulated by the bookkeeping process: financial statements, tax returns, and various confidential reports to managers. Measuring profit is a critical task that accountants perform — a task that depends on the accuracy of the information that the bookkeeper records. The accountant decides how to measure sales revenue and expenses to determine the profit or loss for the period. The tough questions about profit — how to measure it in today's complex and advanced economic environment, and what profit consists of — can't be answered through book-keeping alone.

The Bookkeeping Cycle

Figure 2-1 presents an overview of the bookkeeping cycle side-by-side with elements of the accounting system. You can follow the basic bookkeeping steps down the left side. The accounting elements are shown in the right column.

The basic steps in the bookkeeping sequence, explained briefly, are as follows. (See also "Bookkeeping and Accounting System Management," later in this chapter, for more details on some of these steps.)

1. **Prepare source documents for all transactions, operations, and other business events; source documents are the starting point in the bookkeeping process.**

   When buying products, a business gets a *purchase invoice* from the supplier. When borrowing money from the bank, a business signs a promissory *note payable* or a *formal loan agreement*, a copy of which the business keeps. When a customer uses a credit card to buy the business's product, the business gets the credit card slip as evidence of the transaction. When preparing payroll electronic payments, a business depends on *salary rosters* and *time cards*.

Steps in Bookkeeping Cycle	**Accounting Functions**
(1) Identify and prepare source documents for all transactions, operations, activities, and developments that should be recorded.	Design source documents that specify the detailed information to record and which approvals and signs-offs are required.
(2) Enter in source documents financial effects and other relevant details that apply for the transactions and other events.	Establish specific rules and methods for determining the financial effects of transactions and other events.
(3) Make original entries of financial effects of transactions and other events, file source documents, and build accounting database.	Establish formal chart of accounts, both control and subsidiary accounts, in which transactions and events are recorded.
(4) Carry out end-of-period procedures, which includes recording the very important adjusting and correcting entries.	Oversee, review, and approve the end-of-period adjusting and correcting entries, both routine and unusual ones.
(5) Prepare adjusted trial balance, to provide the up-to-date and accurate listing of all accounts at end of period.	Prepare and distribute: > Internal accounting reports to managers > Tax returns to government agencies > External financial statements
(6) Perform closing procedures at end of fiscal year to prepare accounts for next period.	Give final approval to closing the books for the year, and determine whether changes are needed in accounting system.

Figure 2-1: *The basic steps of the bookkeeping cycle, with the corresponding accounting functions*

All of these key business forms and electronic source documents serve as sources of information into the bookkeeping system — in other words, information the bookkeeper uses in recording the financial effects of the business's activities.

2. **Determine and enter in source documents the financial effects of the transactions and other business events.**

   Transactions have financial effects that must be recorded — the business is better off, worse off, or at least "different off" as the result of its transactions. Examples of typical business transactions include paying employees, making sales to customers, borrowing money from the bank, and buying products to sell to customers. The bookkeeping process begins by determining the relevant information about each transaction. The business's chief accountant establishes the rules and methods for measuring the financial effects of transactions. Of course, the bookkeeper should comply with these rules and methods.

3. **Make original entries of financial effects into journals and accounts, with appropriate references to source documents.**

   Using the source document(s) for every transaction, the bookkeeper makes the first, or original, entry into a journal and then into the business's accounts. Only the official, established chart of accounts should be used in recording transactions.

   A *journal* is a chronological record of transactions in the order in which they occur — like a detailed personal diary. In computerized accounting applications, the journal can be shown as a chronological record of transactions but will most often be displayed as a flexible transaction input screen. In contrast, an account is a separate record, or page as it were, for each asset, each liability, and so on. One transaction affects two or more accounts. The journal entry records the entire transaction in one place; then each piece is recorded in the two or more accounts that are affected by the transaction.

A simple example illustrates recording a transaction in a journal and then posting the changes caused by the transaction in the accounts. Expecting a big demand from its customers, a retail bookstore purchases, on credit, 50 copies of an accounting book from the publisher. The books are received and placed on the shelves. The bookstore now owns the books and also owes the publisher $750, which is the cost of the 50 copies. Here you look only at recording the purchase of the books, not recording subsequent sales of the books and paying the bill to the publisher.

The bookstore has established a specific inventory account called "Inventory — Trade Paperbacks" for books like these. And the purchase liability to the publisher should be entered in the account "Accounts Payable — Publishers." So the journal entry for this purchase is recorded as follows:

| Asset: | Inventory — Trade Paperbacks | + $750.00 |
| Liability: | Accounts Payable — Publishers | + $750.00 |

This pair of changes is first recorded in one journal entry or one screen of the accounting program. Each change is posted automatically or recorded in the separate accounts — one an asset and the other a liability.

In ancient days, bookkeepers had to record these entries by hand. Now bookkeepers use computer programs that take over many of the tedious chores of bookkeeping (see the later section "Accounting Software in the Cloud and on the Ground"). The work gets done more quickly and with fewer errors.

The importance of entering transaction data correctly and in a timely manner can't be exaggerated. The prevalence of data entry errors was one important reason why most retailers started to use cash registers that read barcode information on products, which more accurately captures the necessary information and speeds up the data entry.

4. **Perform end-of-period procedures — the critical steps for getting the accounting records up-to-date and ready for the preparation of management accounting reports, tax returns, and financial statements.**

A *period* is a stretch of time — from one day to one month to one quarter (three months) to one year — determined by the business's needs. A year is the longest period of time that a business would wait to prepare its financial statements. Most businesses need accounting reports and financial statements at the end of each quarter, and many need monthly financial statements.

Before the accounting reports can be prepared at the end of the period (refer to Figure 2-1), the book-keeper must bring the business's accounts up-to-date and complete the bookkeeping process. One step, for example, is recording the depreciation expense for the period. (See Chapter 3 for more on depreciation.) Another step is getting an actual count of the business's inventory so that the inventory records can be adjusted to account for shoplifting, employee theft, and other losses.

The accountant needs to take the final step and check for errors in the business's accounts. Data entry clerks and bookkeepers may not fully understand the unusual nature of some business transactions and may have entered transactions incorrectly. One reason for establishing internal controls (discussed later in this chapter) is to keep errors to a minimum. Ideally, accounts should contain very few errors at the end of the period, but the accountant should not make any assumptions and should do a final check for errors that might have fallen through the cracks.

5. **Compile the adjusted trial balance for the accountant, which is the basis for preparing reports, tax returns, and financial statements.**

After all end-of-period procedures have been completed, the bookkeeper compiles a complete listing of all accounts called the *adjusted trial balance,* which is typically computer generated. Modest-sized businesses maintain hundreds of accounts for their various assets, liabilities, owners' equity, revenue, and expenses. Larger businesses keep thousands of accounts, and very large businesses might keep more than 10,000 accounts. In contrast, external financial statements, tax returns, and internal accounting reports to managers contain a relatively small number of line items with amounts. For example, a typical external balance sheet or an income tax return reports only 25 to 30 line items (maybe even fewer).

The accountant takes the adjusted trial balance and groups similar accounts into one summary amount that is reported in a financial report or tax return. For example, a business might keep hundreds of separate inventory accounts, every one of which is listed in the adjusted trial balance. The accountant collapses all these accounts into one summary inventory account that is presented in the business's external balance sheet. In grouping the accounts, the accountant should comply with established financial reporting standards and income tax requirements.

6. *Close the books* — **bring the bookkeeping for the fiscal year just ended to a close and get things ready to begin the bookkeeping process for the coming fiscal year.**

Books is the common term for a business's complete set of accounts. A business's transactions are a constant stream of activities that don't end tidily on the last day of the year, which can make preparing financial statements and tax returns challenging. The business has to draw a clear line of demarcation between activities for the year (the 12-month accounting period) ended and the year yet to come *by* closing the books for one year and starting with fresh books for the next year. The closing process is automated when using a computerized system.

Most medium-size and larger businesses have an *accounting manual* that spells out in great detail the specific accounts and procedures for recording transactions. But all businesses change over time, and they occasionally need to review their accounting system and make revisions. Companies do not take this task lightly; discontinuities in the accounting system can be major shocks and have to be carefully thought out. Nevertheless, bookkeeping and accounting systems can't remain static for very long. If these systems were never changed, bookkeepers would still be sitting on high stools making entries with quill pens and bottled ink in leather-bound ledgers.

Bookkeeping and Accounting System Management

Many business managers and owners ignore their book-keeping and accounting systems or take them for granted — unless something goes wrong. They assume that if the books are in balance, everything is okay. The section "Double-Entry Accounting for Single-Entry Folks," later in this chapter, covers exactly what "books in balance" means — it does *not* necessarily mean that everything is okay.

To determine whether your bookkeeping system is up to snuff, check out the following sections, which provide a checklist of the most important elements of a good system.

Categorize your financial information: The chart of accounts

Suppose you're the accountant for a corporation and you're faced with the daunting task of preparing the annual income tax return for the business. This demands that you report the following kinds of expenses:

- Advertising and promotion
- Bad debts
- Compensation of officers
- Cost of goods sold
- Depreciation and amortization
- Employee benefit costs
- Interest
- Internet and telephone
- Pensions and profit-sharing plans
- Rent
- Repairs and maintenance
- Salaries and wages
- Taxes and licences

You must provide additional information for some of these expenses. For example, the cost of goods sold expense is determined in a schedule that also requires inventory cost at the beginning of the year, purchases during the year, cost of labour during the year (for manufacturers), other costs, and inventory cost at year-end.

Where do you start? Well, if it's December 1 and the tax return deadline is December 31, you start by panicking — unless you were smart enough to think ahead about the kinds of information your business would need to report. In fact, when your accountant first designs your business's accounting system, he or she should dissect every report to managers, the external financial statements, and the tax returns, breaking down all the information into categories such as those we just listed.

For each category, you need an *account,* a record of the activities in that category. An account is basically a focused history of a particular dimension of a business. Individuals can have accounts, too — for example, your chequebook is an account of the cash inflows and outflows and the balance of your chequing account (assuming that you remember to record all activities and reconcile your chequebook against your bank account balance). You probably don't keep a written account of the coin and currency in your wallet, pockets, glove compartment, and sofa cushions, but a business needs to. An account serves as the source of information for preparing financial statements, tax returns, and reports to managers.

The term *general ledger* refers to the complete set of accounts established and maintained by a business. The *chart of accounts* is the formal index of these accounts — the complete listing and classification of the accounts used by the business to record its transactions. *General ledger* usually refers to the accounts and often to the balances in these accounts at some particular time.

The chart of accounts, even for a relatively small business, normally contains 100 or more accounts. Larger business organizations need thousands of accounts. The larger the number, the more likely that the accounts are given number codes according to some scheme — for example, all assets might be in the 100 to 300 range, all liabilities in the 400 to 500 range, and so on.

A business manager should make sure that the controller (chief accountant), or perhaps an outside professional public accountant, reviews the chart of accounts periodically to determine whether the accounts are up-to-date and adequate for the business's needs. Over time, income tax rules change, the company goes into new lines of business, the company adopts new employee benefit plans, or managers want the accounting information prepared in more detail. Most businesses are in constant flux, and the chart of accounts has to keep up with these changes.

Standardize source document forms and procedures

It's said that armies move on their stomachs. Well, businesses move on their paperwork. Placing an order to buy products, selling a product to a customer, determining the earnings of an employee for the month — virtually every business transaction needs paperwork, generally known as source documents. Source documents, including electronic records of those documents, serve as evidence of the terms and conditions agreed upon by the business and the other person or organization that it's dealing with. Both parties receive some kind of source document. For example, for a sale at a cash register, the customer gets a sales receipt, and the business keeps a running tape of all transactions in the cash register.

Clearly, an accounting system needs to standardize the forms and procedures for processing and recording all normal, repetitive transactions and control the generation and handling of these source documents. From the bookkeeping point of view, these business forms and documents are important because they provide the input information needed for recording transactions in the business's accounts. Sloppy paperwork leads to sloppy accounting records, and sloppy accounting records just won't do when the time comes to prepare tax returns and financial statements.

Computer accounting software packages include templates for most business forms and source documents needed by a business. If you're the owner of a small business, you may want to go online to search for examples of the kinds of forms and documents that you can adapt for recording business transactions.

Hire competent, trained personnel

A business shouldn't be penny-wise and pound-foolish: What good is meticulously collecting source documents if the information on those documents isn't entered into your system correctly? You shouldn't try to save a few bucks by hiring the lowest-paid people you can find. Bookkeepers and accountants, like all other employees in a business, should have the skills and knowledge needed to perform their functions.

Here are some guidelines for choosing the right people to enter and control the flow of your business's data and for making sure that those people *remain* the right people.

University or college degree

Many accountants in business organizations have a university or college degree with a major in accounting. However, as you move down the accounting department, you find that more and more employees do not have a degree and perhaps don't even have any courses in accounting — they learned bookkeeping methods and skills through on-the-job training. Although these employees may have good skills and instincts, they tend to do things by the book; they often lack the broader perspective necessary for detecting errors, improvising, and being innovative. So you want to at least look twice at a potential employee who has no university- or college-based accounting background.

CPA

When hiring higher-level accountants in a business organization, determine whether they should hold a professional accounting designation. Most larger businesses insist on this credential, along with a specific number of years' experience in public accounting or in the private sector.

A business is prudent to require a professional designation for its chief accountant (who usually holds the title of *controller*). Or a business should consult regularly with a public accountant for advice on its accounting system — especially regarding how to treat particularly unusual transactions and accounting problems that come up.

Depending on the complexity of the issues that might come up during regular operations, the requirement or need to have someone on staff who holds a professional designation will vary. Having experience in the industry likely is the most valuable asset a candidate brings to the business.

Continuing education

Bookkeepers and accountants need continuing education to keep up with changes in the income tax law and financial reporting requirements, as well as changes in how the business operates. Ideally, bookkeepers and accountants are able to spot needed improvements and implement these changes — to make accounting reports to managers more useful, for example.

Fortunately, many short-term courses, home-study programs, and the like are available at reasonable costs for keeping up on the latest accounting developments. Many continuing education courses are available on the Internet, but be sure to check out the standards of an Internet course.

CPA Canada requires members to stay up-to-date on professional development to keep their memberships in good standing. Structured activities such as advanced post-secondary education courses or unstructured learning such as on-the-job training or technical research would qualify for this requirement. What is essential is that the activity be relevant and appropriate to the accountant's work and professional responsibilities, and that it contains significant intellectual or practical content.

For example, the CPA Ontario's requirements for CPAs include the completion of *continuing professional development* (CPD) activities. The minimum requirement is 120 hours for a three-year period with 50 percent that is verifiable. Licensed accounting practitioners are subject to an additional level of scrutiny of their professional work. Mandatory practice inspection ensures that their work is done in accordance with the professional standards. All licensed accounting practitioners must also purchase liability insurance. These rules are in place to protect the public's interest.

Integrity

What's possibly the most important quality to look for is also the hardest to judge. Bookkeepers and accountants need to be honest people because of the control they have over your business's financial records. Conduct a careful background check when hiring new accounting personnel and ensure that they can be bonded.

After you hire them, periodically (and discreetly) check whether their lifestyles match their salaries. Small-business owners and managers have closer day-in and day-out contact with their accountants and bookkeepers, which can be an advantage — they get to know their accountants and bookkeepers on a personal level. Even so, you can find many cases where a trusted bookkeeper has embezzled many thousands of dollars over the years. There are many true stories about long-time, "trusted" bookkeepers who made off with some of the family fortune.

Enforce strong internal controls

Any accounting system worth its salt should establish and vigorously enforce effective *internal controls* — basically, additional forms and procedures over and above what's needed strictly to move operations along. These additional procedures serve to deter and detect errors (honest mistakes) and all forms of dishonesty by employees, customers, suppliers, and even managers themselves. Unfortunately, many businesses pay only lip service to internal controls; they don't put into place good internal controls, or they don't seriously enforce their internal controls (they just go through the motions).

Internal controls are like highway truck weigh stations, which make sure that a truck's load doesn't exceed the limits and that the truck has a valid plate. You're just checking that your staff is playing by the rules. For example, to prevent or minimize shoplifting, most retailers now have video surveillance, as well as tags that set off alarms if the customer leaves the store with the tag still on the product. Likewise, a business should implement certain procedures and forms to prevent (as much as possible) theft, embezzlement, kickbacks, fraud, and simple mistakes by its own employees and managers.

Do the names Enron and Nortel ring a bell? Regulatory changes have been put in place to try to prevent accounting scandals. In the United States, passage of the federal Sarbanes-Oxley Act (SOX) of 2002 put even more demands on organizations' internal controls. SOX imposes new responsibilities on top-level executives to make sure the controls are in place and working well. SOX regulations apply not only to businesses operating in the United States but also to businesses owned by U.S. companies that operate in other countries, including Canada. Although the law applies only to public companies, some accountants worry that the requirements of the law will have a trickle-down effect on smaller private businesses as well.

In Canada, many public companies — such as all of our national banks — have their shares traded on the New York Stock Exchange or NASDAQ. Consequently, the SOX rules with respect to corporate governance, enhanced financial disclosures, auditors' independence, and so on apply to the Canadian companies in the same way.

Other, non-public businesses that rely on external sources of financing generally don't wait to be told by a governing body how to strengthen their financial reporting. They see the writing on the wall. Most implement the more rigorous governance and other rules before the government mandates them. They prefer to be viewed as progressive businesses above reproach. They immediately implemented detailed procedures and extra controls similar to those mandated in the United States through SOX. They want to attract or retain continued confidence of the owners and creditors.

Not-for-profit organizations pay particular attention to the public's perception of their financial reporting and integrity. They rely heavily on government grants and private donations to fund their activities. Governments have implemented additional internal control procedures and reporting guidelines, which in turn have trickled down to the organizations that benefit directly from government funding.

Smaller businesses tend to think that they're immune to embezzlement and fraud by their loyal and trusted employees. These are personal friends, after all. Yet many small businesses are hit hard by fraud and usually can least afford the consequences. Most studies of fraud in small businesses have found that the average loss is well into six figures. Even in a friendly game of poker, people always cut the deck before dealing the cards around the table. Your business, too, should put checks and balances into place to discourage dishonest practices and to uncover any fraud and theft as soon as possible.

And then there's the growing specter of hacks into the information databases of businesses. These intrusions are referred to as *cyberthreats*. Hackers have broken into the computer information systems of many major companies, getting around the inadequate controls the businesses had in place. Interestingly, hackers haven't shown interest in accounting information per se. Rather, the hackers are after Social Insurance numbers, credit scores, home addresses, passwords, email addresses — mainly personal and private information.

There is no known computer database break-in for the purpose of manipulating or destroying accounting information — but a hacker could alter accounting information after breaking into a company's information system. The topic of cybercrime is beyond the scope of this book, other than to warn you about this serious threat that requires a new set of internal controls. A class of forensic professionals has emerged who advise and assist businesses in coming to grips with cyberthreats. These specialists include both accountants and IT (information technology) experts.

Complete the process with end-of-period procedures

Suppose that all transactions during the year have been recorded correctly. Therefore, the business's accounts are ready for preparing its financial statements, aren't they? Not so fast!

Certain additional procedures are necessary at the end of the period to bring the accounts up to snuff for preparing financial statements for the year. Two main things have to be done at the end of the period:

- **Record normal, routine *adjusting entries:*** For example, depreciation expense isn't a transaction as such and therefore isn't included in the flow of transactions recorded in the day-to-day bookkeeping process. (Chapter 3 explains depreciation expense.) Similarly, certain other expenses and income may not have been associated with a specific transaction and, therefore, have not been recorded. These kinds of adjustments are necessary to have correct balances for determining profit for the period, and to make the revenue, gain, expense, and loss accounts up-to-date and correct for the year.

- **Make a careful sweep of all matters** *to check for other developments that may affect the accuracy of the accounts:* For example, the company may have discontinued a product line. The remaining inventory of these products may have to be removed from the asset account, with a corresponding loss recorded in the period. Or the company may have settled a long-standing lawsuit, and the amount of damages needs to be recorded. Layoffs and severance packages are another example of what the chief accountant needs to look for before preparing reports.

Lest you still think of accounting as dry and dull, note that end-of-period accounting procedures can stir up heated debates. These procedures require that the accountant make decisions and judgment calls that upper management might not agree with. For example, the accountant might suggest recording major losses that would put a big dent in profit for the year or cause the business to report an overall loss. The outside auditor (assuming that the business has an independent audit of its financial statements) often gets in the middle of the argument. These kinds of debates are precisely why business managers need to know some accounting: to hold up their end of the argument.

Leave good audit trails

Good bookkeeping systems leave good audit trails. An *audit trail* is a clear-cut path of the sequence of events leading up to an entry in the accounts. An accountant starts with the source documents and follows through the bookkeeping steps in recording transactions to reconstruct this path. Even if a business doesn't have an outside public accountant do an annual audit, the accountant has frequent occasion to go back to the source documents and either verify certain information in the accounts or reconstruct the information in a different manner. Suppose that a salesperson claims some suspicious-looking travel expenses; the accountant would probably want to go through all this person's travel and entertainment reimbursements for the past year.

If the Canada Revenue Agency (CRA) comes in for a field audit of your business, you'd better have good audit trails to substantiate all your expense deductions and sales revenue for the year. The CRA has rules about saving source documents for a reasonable period of time and having a well-defined process for making bookkeeping entries and keeping accounts. Think twice before throwing away source documents too soon.

Also, ask your accountant to demonstrate and lay out for your inspection the audit trails for key transactions, such as cash collections, sales, cash disbursements, and inventory purchases. Even computer-based accounting systems recognize the importance of audit trails. Well-designed computer programs provide the capability to backtrack through the sequence of steps in the recording of specific transactions.

Look out for unusual events and developments

Business managers should encourage their accountants to be alert to anything out of the ordinary that might require attention. Suppose the accounts receivable balance for a customer is rapidly increasing — that is, the customer is buying more and more from your company on credit but isn't paying for these purchases on time. Maybe the customer has switched more of his company's purchases to your business and is buying more from you only because he is buying less from other businesses. But maybe the customer is planning to stiff your business and take off without paying his debts. Or maybe the customer is planning to go into bankruptcy soon and is stockpiling products before the company's credit rating heads south.

Don't forget internal time bombs: A bookkeeper's reluctance to take a vacation could mean that she doesn't want anyone else looking at the books.

To some extent, accountants have to act as the business's eyes and ears. Of course, that's one of the main functions of a business manager as well, but the accounting staff can play an important role.

Design truly useful reports for managers

Managers have received too many off-the-mark accounting reports — reports that are difficult to decipher and not very useful or relevant to the manager's decision-making needs and control functions.

Part of the problem lies with the managers themselves. As a business manager, have you told your accounting staff what you need to know, when you need it, and how to present it in the most efficient manner? When you stepped into your position, you probably didn't hesitate to rearrange your office, and maybe you even insisted on hiring your own support staff. Yet you most likely lay down like a lapdog regarding your accounting reports. Maybe you assume that the reports have to be done a certain way and that arguing for change is no use.

On the other hand, accountants bear a good share of the blame for poor management reports. Accountants should proactively study the manager's decision-making responsibilities and provide the information that is most useful, presented in the most easily digestible manner.

In designing the chart of accounts, the accountant should keep in mind the type of information needed for management reports. To exercise control, managers need much more detail than what's reported on tax returns and external financial statements. And expenses should be regrouped into different categories for management decision-making analysis. A good chart of accounts looks to both the external and the internal (management) needs for information.

 So what's the answer for a manager who receives poorly formatted reports? Demand a report format that suits your needs!

Double-Entry Accounting for Single-Entry Folks

Businesses and not-for-profit entities use *double-entry accounting*. But who knows any individual who uses double-entry accounting in personal bookkeeping? Instead, individuals use single-entry accounting.

For example, when you make a payment, either by cheque or by an online bank payment on your credit card balance, you make an entry to decrease your bank balance. And that's it. It wouldn't occur to you to make a second, companion entry to decrease your credit card liability balance. Why? Because you don't keep a liability account for what you owe on your credit card. You depend on the credit card company to make an entry to decrease your balance.

Businesses and not-for-profit entities have to keep track of their liabilities as well as their assets. And they have to keep track of *all* sources of their assets. (Some part of their total assets comes from money invested by their owners, for example.) When a business writes a cheque to pay one of its liabilities, it makes a two-sided (or double) entry — one to decrease its cash balance and the second to decrease the liability. This is double-entry accounting in action. Double-entry does *not* mean a transaction is recorded twice; it means both sides of the transaction are recorded at the same time.

Double-entry accounting pivots off the accounting equation: Total assets = Total liabilities + Total owners' equity

The accounting equation is a condensed version of the balance sheet. The balance sheet is the financial statement that summarizes a business's assets on the one side and its liabilities plus its owners' equity on the other side. Liabilities and owners' equity are the sources of its assets. Each source has different claims on the assets, which are explained in Chapter 4.

One main function of the bookkeeping system is to record all transactions of a business — every single last one. If you look at transactions through the lens of the accounting equation, they have a beautiful symmetry (well, beautiful to accountants at least). All transactions have a natural balance. The sum of financial effects on one side of a transaction equals the sum of financial effects on the other side.

Suppose a business buys a new delivery truck for $65,000 and pays by cheque. The truck asset account increases by the $65,000 cost of the truck, and cash decreases $65,000. Here's another example: A company borrows $2 million from its bank. Its cash increases $2 million, and the liability for its loan payable to the bank increases the same amount.

Just one more example: Suppose a business suffers a loss from a tornado because some of its assets were not insured. The assets destroyed by the tornado are written off (decreased to zero balances), and the amount of the loss decreases owners' equity the same amount. The loss works its way through the income statement but ends up as a decrease in owners' equity.

Virtually all business bookkeeping systems use *debits and credits* for making sure that both sides of transactions are recorded and for keeping the two sides of the accounting equation in balance. A change in an account is recorded as either a debit or a credit according to the following rules:

Assets	= Liabilities	+ Owners' Equity
+ Debit	+ Credit	+ Credit
– Credit	– Debit	– Debit

An increase in an asset is tagged as a debit; an increase in a liability or owners' equity account is tagged as a credit. Decreases are just the reverse. Following this scheme, the total of debits must equal the total of credits in recording every transaction. In brief: *Debits must equal credits.* Debits and credits have been used for centuries.

Note: Sales revenue and expense accounts also follow debit and credit rules. Revenue increases owners' equity (thus is a credit), and an expense decreases owners' equity (thus is a debit).

The *balance* in an account at a point in time equals the increases less the decreases recorded in the account. Following the rules of debits and credits, asset accounts have debit balances, and liabilities and owners' equity accounts have credit balances. (Yes, a balance sheet account can have a wrong-way balance in unusual situations, such as cash having a credit balance because the business has written more cheques than it has in its chequing account.) The total of accounts with debit balances should equal the total of accounts with credit balances.

When the total of debit balance accounts equals the total of credit balance accounts, the *books are in balance.*

Balanced books don't necessarily mean that all accounts have correct balances. Errors are still possible. The bookkeeper might have recorded debits or credits in wrong accounts, or might have entered wrong amounts, or might have missed recording some transactions altogether. Having balanced books simply means that the total of accounts with debit balances equals the total of accounts with credit balances. The important thing is whether the books (the accounts) have *correct* balances, which depends on whether all transactions and other developments have been recorded correctly.

Accounting Software in the Cloud and on the Ground

Although it's not likely, a small business could keep its books the old-fashioned way: making handwritten entries or using Excel. However, even a small business has a relatively large number of transactions that have to be recorded in journals and accounts, to say nothing about the end-of-period steps in the bookkeeping cycle (refer to Figure 2-1).

Many businesses do their accounting work in-house, on the ground at its own location. They use on-the-premises computers, develop or buy accounting software, and control their own backup files. They might use an outside firm to handle certain accounting chores, particularly payroll.

Alternatively, a business can do some or most of its accounting in the cloud. The term *cloud* refers to large-scale offsite computer servers that a business connects with over the Internet. The cloud can be used simply as the backup storage location for the company's accounting records. Cloud servers have the reputation of being difficult to break into by hackers. Of course, the business still needs strong controls over the transmission of accounting information to and from the cloud.

Accounting software packages exist for every size of business, from small (say, $5 million annual sales or less and 20 employees or fewer) to very large ($500 million annual sales and up and 500 employees or more). Developing and marketing accounting software is a booming business. You could do a Google search for *accounting software*, but be prepared for many, many results. Except for larger entities that employ their own accounting software and information technology experts, most businesses need the advice and help of outside consultants in choosing, implementing, upgrading, and replacing accounting software.

Here are some words of wisdom about accounting software:

- Choose your accounting software carefully. Pulling up stakes and switching to another software package is hard. Changing even one module in your accounting software can be difficult.

- In evaluating accounting software, you and your accountant should consider three main factors: ease of use, whether it has the particular features and functionality you need, and the likelihood that the vendor will continue in business and be around to update and make improvements in the software.

- In real estate, the prime concern is "location, location, location." The watchwords in accounting software are "security, security, security." You need tight controls over all aspects of using the accounting software, especially who is authorized to make changes in any of the accounting software modules.

- Although accounting software offers the opportunity to exploit your accounting information (mine the data), you have to know exactly what to look for. The software does not do this automatically. You have to ask for the exact type of information you want and insist that it be pulled out of the accounting data.

- Even when using advanced, sophisticated accounting software, a business has to design the specialized reports it needs for its various managers and make sure that these reports are generated correctly from the accounting database.

- Never forget the "garbage in, garbage out" rule. Data entry errors can be a serious problem in computer-based accounting systems. You can minimize these input errors, but it is next to impossible to eliminate them. Even barcode readers make mistakes, and the barcode tags themselves might have been tampered with. Strong internal controls for the verification of data entry are extremely important.

- Make sure your accounting software leaves good audit trails, which you need for management control, for your auditor when auditing your financial statements, and for the CRA when it decides to audit your income tax returns. The CRA considers the lack of good audit trails suspicious.

- Online accounting systems that permit remote input and access over the Internet or a local area network with multiple users present special security problems. Think twice before putting your accounting system online.

Smaller businesses, and even many medium-size businesses, don't have the budget to hire full-time information system and information technology specialists. They use consultants to help them select accounting software packages, install software, and get it up and running. Like other computer software, accounting programs are frequently revised and updated. A consultant can help keep a business's accounting software up-to-date, correct flaws and security weaknesses in the program, and take advantage of its latest features.

3

Revenue, Expenses, and the Bottom Line

This chapter lifts up the hood and explains how the profit engine runs. Making a profit is the main financial goal of a business. (Not-for-profit organizations and government entities don't aim to make profit, but they should at least avoid overall losses.) Accountants are the designated financial scorekeepers in the business world. Accountants are professional profit-measurers.

Making a profit and accounting for it aren't nearly as simple as you may think. Managers have the demanding tasks of making sales and controlling expenses, and accountants have the tough tasks of measuring revenue and expenses and preparing reports that summarize the profit-making activities.

Also, accountants help business managers analyze profit for decision making and prepare profit budgets for managers.

This chapter focuses on the financial consequences of making profit and how profit activities are reported in a business's external financial reports to its owners and lenders. GAAP (generally accepted accounting principles) governs the recording and reporting of profit; see Chapter 1 for details about GAAP.

A Typical Income Statement

At the risk of oversimplification, you can say that businesses make profit three basic ways:

- Selling *products* (with allied services) and controlling the cost of the products sold and other operating costs

- Selling *services* and controlling the cost of providing the services and other operating costs

- *Investing* in assets that generate investment income and market value gains and controlling operating costs

Obviously, this list isn't exhaustive, but it captures a large slice of business activity. This chapter concentrates on the first category of activity: selling products. Products range from automobiles to computers to food to clothes to jewellery.

The customers of a business may be the final consumers in the economic chain, or a business may sell to other businesses.

Businesses that sell products

Figure 3-1 presents a typical profit report for a product-oriented business; this report, called the *income statement*, would be sent to its outside owners and lenders. The report could just as easily be called the *net income statement* because the bottom-line profit term preferred by accountants is *net income*, but the word *net* is dropped off the title.

Typical Product Business, Inc. Income Statement For Year Ended December 31, 2020	
Sales Revenue	$26,000,000
Cost of Goods Sold Expense	14,300,000
Gross Margin	11,700,000
Selling, General, and Administrative Expenses	8,700,000
Operating Earnings	3,000,000
Interest Expense	400,000
Earnings Before Income Tax	2,600,000
Income Tax Expense	910,000
Net Income	$1,690,000
Earnings Per Share	$3.38

Figure 3-1: *Typical income statement for a business that sells products*

Alternative titles for the external profit report include *statement of financial performance, earnings statement, operating statement, statement of operating results,* and *statement of earnings.* (Note that profit reports distributed to managers inside a business are usually called *P&L* [profit and loss] statements, but this moniker is not used in external financial reporting.)

The heading of an income statement identifies the business (which in this example is incorporated — thus the term "Inc." following the name), the financial statement title ("Income Statement"), and the time period summarized by the statement ("Year Ended December 31, 2020").

You may be tempted to start reading an income statement at the bottom line. But this financial report is designed to be read from the top line (sales revenue) down to the last — the bottom line (net income). Each step down the ladder in an income statement involves the deduction of an expense. In Figure 3-1, four expenses are deducted from the sales revenue amount, and four profit lines are given: gross margin, also often called gross profit; operating earnings; earnings before income tax; and net income:

- **Gross margin (also called gross profit):** Sales revenue minus the cost of goods (products) sold expense but before operating and other expenses are considered

- **Operating earnings (or loss):** Profit (or loss) before interest and income tax expenses are deducted from gross margin

- **Earnings (or loss) before income tax:** Profit (or loss) after deducting interest expense from operating earnings but before income tax expense

- **Net income:** Final profit for the period after deducting all expenses from sales revenue, which is commonly called the *bottom line*

Although you see income statements with fewer than four profit lines, you seldom see an income statement with more.

The terminology in income statements varies from business to business, but you can usually determine the meaning of a term from its context and placement in the income statement.

Note in Figure 3-1 that below the net income line, the *earnings per share* (EPS) amount is reported. This important number equals net income divided by the number of ownership shares that the business corporation has issued and that are being held by its shareholders. All public corporations whose shares are traded in stock markets must report this key metric. EPS is compared to the current market price of the share to help judge whether the share is overpriced or underpriced. Private companies aren't required to report EPS, but they may decide to do so. If a private business decides to report its EPS, it should follow the accounting standard for calculating this number.

The standard practice for almost all businesses is to report two-year comparative financial statements in side-by-side columns — for the period just ended and for the same period one year ago. Some companies present three-year comparative financial statements. Two-year or three-year financial statements may be legally required, such as for public companies whose debt and shares are traded in a public market. Note that the income statement in Figure 3-1 is incomplete in this regard. It should have a companion column for the year ending December 31, 2019.

Businesses that sell services

Figure 3-2 presents a typical income statement for a service-oriented business. The sales revenue and operating earnings are the same amount for both the product and the service businesses so you could more easily compare the two.

If a business sells services and does not sell products, it does not have a cost of goods sold expense; therefore, the company does not show a gross margin line. Note that you'll find many variations on the basic income statement example in Figure 3-2. In particular, a business has a fair amount of latitude regarding the number of expense lines to disclose in its external income statement.

Typical Service Business, Inc. Income Statement For Year Ended December 31, 2020	
Service Revenue	$26,000,000
Marketing and Selling Expenses	4,325,000
Operating and Administrative Expenses	8,700,000
Employee Compensation Expense	9,975,000
Operating Earnings	3,000,000
Interest Expense	200,000
Earnings Before Income Tax	2,800,000
Income Tax Expense	980,000
Net Income	$1,820,000
Earnings Per Share	$3.64

Figure 3-2: *Typical income statement for a business that sells services*

In Figure 3-2, the first profit line is *operating earnings*, which is profit before interest and income tax. The service business example in Figure 3-2 discloses three broad types of expenses. You might have noticed that the interest expense for the service business is lower than for the product business (compare with Figure 3-1). Therefore, the service business has higher earnings before income tax and higher net income and EPS.

The premise of financial reporting is that of *adequate disclosure*, but you find many variations in the reporting of expenses. A business — whether a product or service company— has wide latitude regarding the number of expense lines to disclose in its external income statement. A CPA auditor (assuming the company's financial report is audited) may not be satisfied that just a few expenses provide enough detail about the operating activities of the business. Accounting standards do not dictate that particular expenses must be disclosed.

Some housekeeping details

Accountants assume everyone knows a few things about income statements, but these things are not obvious to many people. (Accountants frequently assume that the people using financial statements know a good deal about the customs and conventions of financial reporting, so they don't make things as clear as they could.) For an accountant, the following facts are second-nature:

- **Minus signs are missing.** Expenses are deductions from sales revenue, but you rarely see minus signs in front of expense amounts to indicate that they are deductions. Forget about minus signs in income statements and in other financial statements as well. Sometimes parentheses are put around a deduction to signal that it's a negative number, but that's the most you can expect to see.

- **Your eye is drawn to the bottom line.** Putting a double underline under the final (bottom-line) profit number for emphasis is common practice but not universal. Instead, net income might be shown in bold type.

- **Profit isn't usually called** *profit*. As you see in Figures 3-1 and 3-2, bottom-line profit is called *net income*. Businesses use other terms as well, such as *net earnings* or just *earnings*. This book uses the terms *net income* and *profit* interchangeably.

- **You don't get details about sales revenue.** The sales revenue amount in an income statement is the combined total of all sales during the year. You can't tell how many different sales were made, how many different customers the company sold products to, or how the sales were distributed over the 12 months of the year. (Public companies are required to release quarterly income statements during the year, and they include a special summary of quarter-by-quarter results in their annual financial reports; private businesses may or may not release quarterly sales data.) Sales revenue does not include sales tax and GST/HST that the business collects from its customers and remits to the governments.

Note: In addition to sales revenue from selling products and service revenue from selling services, a business may have income from other sources. For instance, a business may have earnings from investments in marketable securities. In its income statement, investment income goes on a separate line and is not commingled with sales revenue. (The businesses featured in Figures 3-1 and 3-2 do not have investment income.)

- **Gross margin matters.** The *cost of goods sold* expense is the cost of products sold to customers, the sales revenue of which is reported on the *sales revenue* line. The idea is to match up the sales revenue of goods sold with the cost of goods sold and show the *gross margin* (also called *gross profit*), which is the profit before other expenses are deducted. The other expenses could in total be more than gross margin, in which case the business would have a loss for the period.

  Note: Companies that sell services rather than products (such as airlines, movie theatres, and accounting firms) do not have a cost of goods sold expense line in their income statements.

- **Operating costs are lumped together.** The broad category *selling, general, and administrative expenses* (refer to Figure 3-1) consists of a wide variety of costs of operating a business and making sales. Some examples follow: labour costs (wages, salaries, and benefits paid to employees); insurance premiums; property taxes on buildings and land; cost of gas and electric utilities; travel and entertainment costs; telephone and Internet charges; depreciation and amortization of operating assets that are used more than one year (including buildings, land improvements, cars and trucks, computers, office furniture, tools and machinery, and shelving); advertising and sales promotion expenditures; and legal and audit costs.

As with sales revenue, you don't get much detail about operating expenses in a typical income statement as it's presented to the company's debtholders and shareholders. A business may disclose more information than you see in its income statement — mainly in the notes that are included with its financial statements.

Your job: Asking questions

The worst thing you can do when presented with an income statement is to be a passive reader. You should be inquisitive. An income statement is not fulfilling its purpose unless you grab it by its numbers and start asking questions.

For example, you should be curious regarding the business's size. Another question to ask is: How does profit compare with sales revenue for the year? Profit (net income) equals what's left over from sales revenue after you deduct all expenses. The business featured in Figure 3-1 squeezed $1.69 million profit from its $26 million sales revenue for the year, which equals 6.5 percent. This ratio of profit to sales revenue, often referred to as *profit margin,* means expenses absorbed 93.5 percent of sales revenue. Although it may seem rather thin, a 6.5 percent profit margin on sales is quite acceptable for many businesses. (Some businesses consistently make a bottom-line profit of 10 to 20 percent of sales, and others are satisfied with a 1 or 2 percent profit margin on sales revenue.) Profit ratios on sales vary widely from industry to industry.

GAAP is relatively silent regarding which expenses have to be disclosed on the face of an income statement or elsewhere in a financial report. For example, the amount a business spends on advertising does not have to be disclosed. On the other hand, GAAP requires disclosure of certain expenses, such as amortization and depreciation as well as interest and income tax expense on the income statement or in the notes to the financial statements.

In the example shown in Figure 3-1, expenses such as labour costs and advertising expenditures are buried in the all-inclusive *selling, general, and administrative expenses* line. (If the business manufactures the products it sells instead of buying them from another business, a good part of its annual labour cost is included in its *cost of goods sold* expense line.) Some companies disclose specific expenses such as advertising and marketing costs, research and development costs, and other significant expenses. In short, income statement expense disclosure practices vary considerably from business to business.

Another set of questions you should ask in reading an income statement concerns the business's *profit performance*. Refer again to the company's profit performance report (see Figure 3-1). Profit-wise, how did the business do? Underneath this question is the implicit question: Relative to what? Generally speaking, three sorts of benchmarks are used for evaluating profit performance:

- Comparisons with broad, industry-wide performance averages
- Comparisons with immediate competitors' performances
- Comparisons with the business's performance in recent years

How to Deconstruct Profit

After you've had the opportunity to read an income statement (see Figures 3-1 and 3-2), here's a question for you:

What *is* profit? Your answer is probably "Profit is revenue less expenses." That answer is correct, as far as it goes, but it doesn't go far enough. It doesn't tell you what profit consists of.

This section explains the anatomy of profit. Having read the product company's income statement, you now know that the business earned net income for the year ending December 31, 2020 (see Figure 3-1). Where's the profit? If you had to put your finger on the profit, where would you touch?

Recording profit works like a pair of scissors: You have a positive revenue blade and a negative expenses blade. Revenue and expenses have opposite effects. This leads to two questions: What is a revenue? And what is an expense?

Figure 3-3 summarizes the financial natures of revenue and expenses in terms of effects on assets and liabilities. Note the symmetrical framework of revenue and expenses. This summary framework is helpful for understanding the financial effects of revenue and expenses.

	Asset	**Liability**
Revenue	+	–
Expense	–	+

Figure 3-3: *Fundamental nature of revenue and expenses*

Revenue and expense effects on assets and liabilities

Here's the gist of the two-by-two matrix shown in Figure 3-3. In recording a sale, the bookkeeper increases a revenue account.

The revenue account accumulates sale after sale during the period. So at the end of the period, the total sales revenue for the period is the balance in the account. This amount is the cumulative end-of-period total of all sales during the period. All sales revenue accounts are combined for the period, and one grand total is reported in the income statement on the top line. As each sale (or other type of revenue event) is recorded, either an asset account is increased or a liability account is decreased.

Revenue increases an asset. For example, if all sales are made for cash, the company's cash account increases accordingly. However, you may have trouble understanding that certain revenue transactions are recorded with a decrease in a liability. Here's why: Customers may pay in advance for a product or service to be delivered later (examples are prepaying for theatre or airline tickets and making a down payment for future delivery of products). In recording such advance payments from customers, the business increases cash, of course, and increases a liability account usually called *unearned revenue* or *deferred revenue*. The term *deferred* simply means postponed. When the product or service is delivered to the customer — and not before then — the bookkeeper records the amount of revenue that has now been earned *and* decreases the unearned revenue liability by the same amount.

Recording expenses is straightforward. When an expense is recorded, a specific expense account is increased, and either an asset account is decreased or a liability account is increased the same amount. For example, to record the cost of goods sold, the expense with this name is increased, say, $35,000, and in the same entry, the inventory asset account is decreased $35,000. Alternatively, an expense entry may involve a liability account instead of an asset account. For example, suppose the business receives a $10,000 bill from its CPA auditor that it will pay later. In recording the bill from the CPA, the audit expense account is increased $10,000 and a liability account called *accounts payable* is increased $10,000.

The summary framework of Figure 3-3 has no exceptions. Recording revenue and expenses (as well as gains and losses) always follows these rules. So where does this leave you for understanding profit? Profit itself doesn't show up in Figure 3-3, does it? Profit depends on amounts recorded for revenue and expenses.

Revenue and expenses are originally recorded as increases or decreases in different asset and liability accounts. Cash is just one asset. The other assets and the liabilities are explained in the later section "Assets and Liabilities Used to Record Revenue and Expenses."

Some businesses make sales for cash; cash is received at the time of the sale. In recording these sales, a revenue account is increased and the cash account is increased. Some expenses are recorded at the time of cutting a cheque to pay the expense.

In recording these expenses, an appropriate expense account is increased and the cash asset account is decreased. However, for most businesses, the majority of their revenue and expense transactions do not simultaneously affect cash.

For most businesses, cash comes into play before or after revenue and expenses are recorded. For example, a business buys product from its supplier that it will sell sometime later to its customers. The purchase is paid for before the goods are sold. No expense is recorded until products are sold. Here's another example: A business makes sales on credit to its customers. In recording credit sales, a sales revenue account is increased and an asset account called *accounts receivable* is increased. Sometime later, the receivables are collected in cash. The amount of cash actually collected through the end of the period may be less than the amount of sales revenue recorded.

Cash inflow from revenue is almost always different from revenue for the period. Furthermore, cash outflow for expenses is almost always different from expenses for the period. The lesson is this: Do not equate revenue with cash inflow, and do not equate expenses with cash outflows. The net cash flow from profit for the period — revenue inflow minus expense outflow — is bound to be higher or lower than the accounting-based measure of profit for the period. The income statement does not report cash flows.

This chapter lays the foundation for Chapter 5, which explains cash flow from profit. Cash flow is an enormously important topic in every business. Even Apple, with its huge treasure of marketable investments, worries about its cash flow.

Profit folded into retained earnings

The business in the Figure 3-1 example earned $1.69 million profit for the year. Therefore, its retained earnings account increased this amount because the bottom-line amount of net income for the period is recorded in this account. You know this for sure. But what you can't tell from the income statement is how the business's assets and liabilities were affected by its sale and expense activities during the period. One possible scenario is the following (in thousands of dollars):

		Owners' equity	
Assets	= Liabilities +	Invested capital +	Retained earnings
+$1,990	= +$300		+$1,690

This scenario works because the sum of the right-side changes ($300,000 increase in liabilities plus $1.69 million increase in retained earnings) equals the $1.99 million increase in assets.

After profit is determined for the period, which means that all revenue and expenses have been recorded for the period, the profit amount is entered as an increase in *retained earnings*. The $1.69 million net income for the year (refer to Figure 3-1) gets closed into retained earnings. Doing this keeps the accounting equation in balance.

In most situations, not all annual profit is distributed to owners; some is retained in the business. Unfortunately, the retained earnings account sounds like an asset in the minds of many people. It isn't. It's a source-of-assets account, not an asset account. It's on the right side of the accounting equation; assets are on the left side.

To summarize, the company's $1.69 million net income resulted in some combination of changes in its assets and liabilities, such that its shareholders' equity (specifically, its retained earnings) increased $1.69 million.

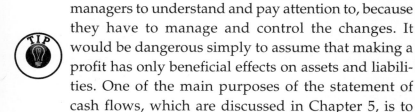

The financial shift in assets and liabilities from profit-making activities is especially important for business managers to understand and pay attention to, because they have to manage and control the changes. It would be dangerous simply to assume that making a profit has only beneficial effects on assets and liabilities. One of the main purposes of the statement of cash flows, which are discussed in Chapter 5, is to summarize the financial changes caused by the business's profit activities during the year.

Assets and Liabilities Used to Record Revenue and Expenses

The sales and expense activities of a business involve inflows and outflows of cash, as you know. What you may not know, however, is that the profit-making process also involves four other basic operating assets and three basic types of operating liabilities. Cash is the pivotal asset. Revenue and expenses, sooner or later, lead to cash. But in the meantime, other asset and liability accounts are used to record the flow of profit activity. Each of the following sections explains the main assets and liabilities used in recording revenue and expenses, which will give you a more realistic picture of what's involved in making profit.

Making sales: Accounts receivable and unearned revenue

Many businesses allow their customers to buy their products or services on credit. They use an asset account called *accounts receivable* to record the total amount owed to the business by its customers who have made purchases "on the cuff" and haven't paid yet. In most cases, a business doesn't collect all its receivables by the end of the year, especially for credit sales that occur in the last weeks of the year. It records the sales revenue and the cost of goods sold expense for these sales as soon as a sale is completed and products are delivered to the customers. This is one feature of the *accrual basis of accounting,* which records revenue when sales are made and records expenses when these costs are incurred. When sales are made on credit, the accounts receivable asset account is increased; later, when cash is received from the customer, cash is increased and the accounts receivable account is decreased. Collecting the cash is the follow-up transaction trailing along after the sale is recorded.

In contrast to making sales on credit, some businesses collect cash before they deliver their products or services to customers. An example is an airline when you buy and pay for an airline ticket days or weeks ahead of your flight. When a business receives advance payments from customers, it increases cash (of course) and increases a liability account called *unearned revenue.* Sales revenue isn't recorded until the product or service is delivered to the customer. When delivered sales revenue or service revenue is increased, the liability account is decreased, which reflects that part of the liability has been paid down by delivery of the product or service.

Increases or decreases in the asset account *accounts receivable* and the liability account *unearned revenue* affect cash flow during the year of the profit-making activities of the business. Cash flow is explained in Chapter 5. Until then, keep in mind that the balance of accounts receivable at the end of the year is the amount of sales revenue that has not yet been converted into cash. Accounts receivable represents cash waiting in the wings to be collected in the near future, and unearned revenue is the amount of money collected in advance from customers. The two accounts appear in the balance sheet, which is discussed in Chapter 4.

Selling products: Inventory

The *cost of goods sold* is one of the primary expenses of businesses that sell products. (In Figure 3-1, note that this expense is equal to more than half the sales revenue for the year.) This expense is just what its name implies: the cost that a business pays for the products it sells to customers. A business makes profit by setting its sales prices high enough to cover the actual costs of products sold, the costs of operating the business, interest on borrowed money, and income taxes (assuming that the business pays income tax), with something left over for profit.

When the business acquires a product, the cost of the product goes into an *inventory asset* account (and the cost is either deducted from the cash account or added to the accounts payable liability account, depending on whether the business pays with cash or buys on credit). When a customer buys that product, the business transfers the cost of the product from the inventory asset account to the *cost of goods sold* expense account because the product is no longer in the business's inventory; the product has been delivered to the customer.

The first step in the income statement is deducting the cost of goods sold expense from the sales revenue for the goods sold. All businesses that sell products must report the cost of goods sold as a separate expense in their income statements, as you see in Figure 3-1.

A business that sells products needs to have a stock of those products on hand to sell to its customers. This stockpile of goods on the shelves (or in storage space in the backroom) waiting to be sold is called *inventory*. When you drive by an auto dealer and see all the cars, SUVs, and pickup trucks waiting to be sold, keep in mind that these products are inventory. The cost of unsold products (goods held in inventory) is not yet an expense; only after the products are sold does the cost get listed as an expense. In this way, the cost of goods sold expense is correctly matched against the sales revenue from the goods sold. Correctly matching expenses against sales revenue is the essence of accounting for profit.

Prepaying operating costs: Prepaid expenses

Prepaid expenses are the opposite of unpaid expenses. For example, a business buys fire insurance and general liability insurance (in case a customer who slips on a wet floor or is insulted by a careless salesperson sues the business). Insurance premiums must be paid ahead of time, before coverage starts. The premium cost is allocated to expense in the actual period benefited. At the end of the year, the business may be only halfway through the insurance coverage period, so it charges off only half the premium cost as an expense. (For a six-month policy, you charge one-sixth of the premium cost to each of the six months covered.) So at the time the premium is paid, the entire amount is recorded in the prepaid expenses asset account, and for each month of coverage, the appropriate fraction of the cost is transferred to the insurance expense account.

Another example of something initially put in the prepaid expenses asset account occurs when a business pays cash to stock up on office supplies that it may not use for several months. The cost is recorded in the prepaid expenses asset account at the time of purchase; when the supplies are used, the appropriate amount is subtracted from the prepaid expenses asset account and recorded in the office supplies expense account.

Using the prepaid expenses asset account is not so much for the purpose of reporting all the assets of a business, because the balance in the account compared with other assets and total assets is typically small. Rather, using this account is an example of allocating costs to expenses in the period benefited by the costs, which isn't always the same period in which the business pays those costs. The prepayment of these expenses lays the groundwork for continuing operations seamlessly into the next year.

Fixed assets: Depreciation expense

Long-term operating assets that are not held for sale in the ordinary course of business are called *property, plant, and equipment* or *fixed assets;* these include buildings, machinery, office equipment, vehicles, computers and data-processing equipment, and shelving and cabinets. *Depreciation* refers to spreading out the cost of a fixed asset over the years of its useful life to a business, instead of charging the entire cost to expense in the year of purchase. That way, each year of use bears a share of the total cost. For example, autos and light trucks are typically depreciated over five years; the idea is to charge a fraction of the total cost to depreciation expense during each of the five years.

Depreciation is a real expense but not a cash outlay expense in the year it is recorded. The cash outlay occurs when the fixed asset is acquired.

Take another look at the business example in Figure 3-1. From the information supplied in its income statement, you don't know how much depreciation expense the business recorded in 2020. However, as required by GAAP, the notes to its financial statements reveal this amount. In 2020, the business recorded $775,000 depreciation expense. Basically, this expense decreases the book value (the recorded value) of its fixed assets. Chapter 4 goes into more detail regarding how depreciation expense is recorded.

Unpaid expenses: Accounts payable, accrued expenses payable, and income tax payable

A typical business pays many expenses *after* the period in which the expenses are recorded. Following are some common examples:

- A business pays its employees in arrears, which means that at any point in time, wages and salaries are owed to employees.

- A business hires a law firm that does a lot of legal work during the year, but the company doesn't pay the bill until the following year.

- A business matches retirement contributions made by its employees but doesn't pay its share until the following year.

- A business has unpaid bills for telephone and Internet service, gas, electricity, and water that it used during the year.

Accountants use three different types of liability accounts to record a business's unpaid expenses:

- **Accounts payable:** This account is used for items that the business buys on credit and for which it receives an invoice (a bill). For example, your business receives an invoice from its lawyers for legal work done. As soon as you receive the invoice, you record in the accounts payable liability account the amount that you owe. Later, when you pay the invoice, you subtract that amount from the accounts payable account, and your cash goes down by the same amount.

- **Accrued expenses payable:** A business has to make estimates for several unpaid costs at the end of the year because it hasn't yet received invoices for them. Examples of accrued expenses include the following: unpaid wages, unused vacation, and sick days that employees carry over to the following year, which the business has to pay for in the coming year; unpaid bonuses to salespeople; unpaid utility expenses at the end of the year because the utility companies don't necessarily bill the business at the end of every month; the cost of future repairs and part replacements on products that customers have bought and haven't yet returned for repair under warranty; and the daily accumulation of interest on borrowed money that won't be paid until the next interest due date.

Without invoices to refer to, you have to examine your business operations carefully to determine which liabilities of this sort to record.

- **Income tax payable:** This account is used for income taxes that a business still owes to the federal and provincial governments at the end of the year. CRA administers all provincial and territorial corporate income taxes except for the provinces of Quebec and Alberta. The income tax expense for the year is the total amount based on the taxable income for the entire year. Your business may not pay 100 percent of its income tax expense during the year; it may owe a small fraction to the governments at year's end. You record the unpaid amount in the income tax payable account.

Note: A business may be unincorporated and be a *proprietorship* or *partnership*. In that case, its income is taxable in the hands of its owners and so there would be no income tax expense appearing on the income statement. What you need to remember about these types of entities is that they are not persons in the eyes of the law, and so they do not pay any taxes. The owners do. In this case, *unincorporated* means that the business entity is not a corporate person created under the provincial or federal incorporation statutes. When a business has a single owner, it is a *proprietorship*. Whenever there is more than one owner, by definition you would then have a *partnership*.

The Financial Effects of Profit

Business managers should understand not only how to make profit but also the financial effects of making profit. Profit does not simply mean an increase in cash. Sales revenue and expenses affect several assets other than cash and operating liabilities.

Making profit involves additional transactions that are closely allied with sales and expenses. These tightly connected transactions include the following:

- Collecting cash from customers for credit sales made to them, which takes place after recording the sales revenue

- Collecting cash from customers ahead of delivering goods or services and ahead of recordings sales revenue

- Purchasing (or manufacturing) products that are put in inventory and held there until the products are sold sometime later, at which time the cost of products sold is charged to expense to match up with the revenue from the sale

- Paying certain costs in advance of when they are charged to expense

- Paying for products bought on credit and for other items that are not charged to expense until sometime after the purchase

- Paying for expenses that have been recorded sometime earlier

- Making payments to the government for income tax expense that has already been recorded

These *allied transactions* are the "before and after" of recording sales and expense transactions. The allied transactions are not reported as such in a financial statement. However, the allied transactions change assets and liabilities, and they definitely affect cash flow. You find out how the changes in assets and liabilities caused by the allied transactions affect cash flow in Chapter 5.

Other transactions also change the assets, liabilities, and owners' equity of a business, such as borrowing money and buying new fixed assets. These non-revenue and non-expense transactions are reported in the statement of cash flows, explained in Chapter 5.

The Reporting of Gains and Losses

The income statement example shown in Figure 3-1 is a sanitized version as compared with actual income statements in external financial reports. If you took the trouble to read a hundred or so income statements, you'd be surprised at the wide range of things you'd find in these statements. But you would discover one thing for certain: Many businesses report *gains and losses* in addition to their usual revenue, operating income, and expenses. In these situations, the income statement is divided into two sections:

- The first section presents the *ordinary, continuing sales, income, and expense from operations* of the business for the year, as well as gains and losses which are highlighted by headings on the income statement such as *other revenues and gains*, and *other expenses and losses*.

- The second section presents any *discontinued operations* that the business recorded in the year.

Unusual gains and losses

Occasionally, a business will suffer some losses or experience some gains that are not caused by day-to-day operations. These losses or gains might be related to the sale of an investment or even a charge against the business for something over which the business has little or no control. These events are considered outside the business's main operations and yet they clearly must be included on the income statement. These unusual gains and losses are shown separately.

Some additional examples of items that would be listed under unusual gains and losses include the following:

- **Settling lawsuits and other legal actions:** Damages and fines that you pay — as well as damages that you *receive* in a favourable ruling — are unusual gains and losses.

- **Writing down (also called writing off) damaged and impaired assets:** If products become damaged and unsellable, or fixed assets are destroyed unexpectedly, you need to remove these items from the asset accounts. Even when certain assets are in good physical condition, if they lose their capability to generate future sales or other benefits to the business, accounting rules say that the assets have to be taken off the books.

- **Relocating or reorganizing the business:** Some one-time charges are paid by the business to address a major shift in customer demand or tackle an economic downturn.

Discontinued operations

The second section of the income statement that deserves even more prominence is the one for discontinued operations of the business. Some examples of discontinued operations include the following:

- **Selling a segment of the business:** Layoffs require severance pay or trigger early retirement costs; selling the fixed assets of the segment may cause large gains or losses.

- **Abandoning product lines:** When you decide to discontinue selling a line of products, you lose at least some of the money that you paid for obtaining or manufacturing the products, either because you sell the products for less than you paid or because you just dump the products you can't sell. As long as the product line was operated as a separate business segment, the costs connected with the abandonment qualify for treatment as discontinued operations.

According to financial reporting standards (GAAP), which are explained in Chapter 1, a business must make these one-time events very visible in its income statement. So, in addition to the main part of the income statement that reports normal profit activities, a business with discontinued operations must add a second layer to the income statement to disclose these happenings.

If a business has no discontinued operations in the year, its income statement ends with one bottom line, usually called *net income* (which is the situation shown in Figure 3-1). When an income statement includes a second layer, that line becomes a subtotal called *income from continuing operations,* as shown in the following:

Income from continuing operations	$267,000,000
Discontinued operations, net of income taxes	(20,000,000)
Net income	$247,000,000

You will note that discontinued operations are shown net of income taxes. You can therefore tell exactly all of the effects, even that of the taxes, of the decision to discontinue the particular operations.

The Statement of Retained Earnings

This chapter shows you that income is the main source of increase to retained earnings. But other events or transactions can also change this account, which holds the equity belonging to the owners. What if something happens and it's too late to report the transaction on the statement of income? "Too late" means that this event or transaction belongs to an earlier year and that year is already over and done with.

Canadian GAAP deals with addressing changes in accounting policy and correcting errors committed in previous years. Imagine you discover an error in recording the amount of amortization or depreciation in a past year. You might be tempted to charge the current-year income statement with the effect of this error. This would not be allowed under Canadian and international GAAP because the expense of the current year would be incorrect as well. Two wrongs don't make a right, even when intended to correct for a past error.

 Following are the two main items that cannot be recorded to the income statement:

- **Changing accounting policy:** A business may decide to use a different method for recording revenue and expenses than it did in the past, in some cases because the accounting rules (set by the authoritative accounting governing bodies) have changed. Often, the new method requires a business to record a one-time cumulative effect caused by the switch in accounting policy. These special items can be huge. Because the effect of the change must appear on the financial statements as though it had been adopted retroactively as soon as possible, the effect on the previous year's income statement has to be applied to the retained earnings balance, net of any tax effect. It is too late to go to the previous years' income statements because these periods are now closed. Find out more about the closing of the books in Chapter 2.

- **Correcting errors from previous financial reports:** If you or your accountant discovers that a past financial report had an accounting error, you make a catch-up correction entry, which means that you record an increase or decrease as an adjustment to the retained earnings, net of any tax effect. This error has nothing to do with your financial performance this year and therefore should not appear in the current year's income statement.

The statement of retained earnings is the fourth financial statement in the typical set of financial statements. It is sometimes very short. Its purpose is to show what happened to retained earnings in the year, outlining how much profit the business made and also the dividends that the business paid the shareholders. In a way, it is the link between the statement of income and the balance sheet. Because it is so short, a lot of accountants combine it with the statement of income.

The statement of retained earnings is used by private enterprises in Canada. Public companies, following International Financial Reporting Standards (IFRS), use an expanded version of the statement of retained earnings called the *statement of changes in equity*. All information found on a statement of retained earnings is included in the statement of changes in equity, along with the details of any increases or decreases to the public company's other equity accounts for the reporting period.

4

Assets, Liabilities, and Owners' Equity

This chapter explores one of the three primary financial statements that businesses report — the *balance sheet,* which is also called the *statement of financial condition* and the *statement of financial position.* This financial statement is a summary at a point in time of the assets of a business on the one hand, and the liabilities and owners' equity sources of the business on the other hand. It's a two-sided financial statement, which can be condensed in the *accounting equation:*

Assets = Liabilities + Shareholders' equity

The balance sheet may seem to stand alone — like an island to itself — because it's presented on a separate page in a financial report. But keep in mind that the assets and liabilities reported in a balance sheet are the results of the business's activities, or transactions. *Transactions* are economic exchanges between the business and the parties it deals with: customers, employees, vendors, government agencies, and sources of capital. Transactions are the stepping stones from the start-of-the year financial condition to the end-of-the-year financial condition.

Transactions Drive the Balance Sheet

A balance sheet is a snapshot of the financial condition of a business at an instant in time — the most important moment in time being at the end of the last day of the income statement period. This chapter continues using the same business example from Chapter 3. The *fiscal*, or accounting, year of the business ends on December 31. So its balance sheet is prepared at the close of business at midnight December 31. (A company should end its fiscal year at the close of its natural business year or at the close of a calendar quarter — September 30, for example.)

This freeze-frame nature of a balance sheet may make it appear that a balance sheet is static. Nothing is further from the truth. A business does not shut down to prepare its balance sheet. The financial condition of a business is in constant motion because the business's activities go on non-stop.

The activities, or transactions, of a business fall into three basic types:

- **Operating activities:** This category refers to making sales and incurring expenses, and also includes the allied transactions that are part and parcel of making sales and incurring expenses. For example, a business records sales revenue when sales are made on credit, and then, later, records cash collections from customers.

  Another example: A business purchases products that are placed in its inventory (its stock of products awaiting sale), at which time it records an entry for the purchase. The expense (the cost of goods sold) is not recorded until the products are sold to customers.

  Keep in mind that the term *operating activities* includes the allied transactions that precede or are subsequent to the recording of sales and expense transactions.

- **Investing activities:** This term refers to making investments in long-term assets and (eventually) disposing of the assets when the business no longer needs them. The primary examples of investing activities for businesses that sell products and services are *capital expenditures,* which are the amounts spent to modernize, expand, and replace the long-term operating assets of a business.

- **Financing activities:** These activities include securing money from debt and equity sources of capital, returning capital to these sources, and making distributions from profit to owners. Note that distributing profit to owners is treated as a financing transaction, not as a separate category.

Wondering where to find these transactions in a financial report? Sales revenue and expenses, as well as any gains or losses recorded in the period, are reported in the income statement. However, the total flows during the period of the allied transactions connected with sales and expenses aren't reported. For example, the total of cash collections from customers from credit sales made to them isn't reported. The net changes in the assets and liabilities directly involved in operating activities are reported in the statement of cash flows (see Chapter 5). Financing and investing transactions are also found in the statement of cash flows. (Reporting the cash flows from investing and financing activities is one of the main purposes of the statement of cash flows.)

Figure 4-1 shows a summary of changes in assets, liabilities, and owners' equity during the year for the business example introduced in Chapter 3. Note the middle three columns in Figure 4-1, for each of the three basic types of activities of a business:

- One column is for net changes caused by its revenue and expenses and their allied transactions during the year, which collectively are called *operating activities.*

- The second column is for net changes caused by its investing activities during the year.
- The third column is for the net changes caused by its financing activities.

Typical Product Business, Inc.
Statement of Changes in Assets, Liabilities, and Owners' Equity
for Year Ended December 31, 2020
(Dollar amounts in thousands)

	Beginning Balances	Operating Activities	Investing Activities	Financing Activities	Ending Balances
Cash	$2,275	$1,515	($1,275)	($350)	$2,165
Accounts receivable	2,150	450			2,600
Inventory	2,725	725			3,450
Prepaid expenses	525	75			600
Fixed assets, net of depreciation	5,535	(775)	1,275		6,035
Assets	$13,210	$1,990		($350)	$14,850
Accounts payable	$640	$125			$765
Accrued expenses payable	750	150			900
Income tax payable	90	25			115
Interest-bearing debt	6,000			$250	6,250
O.E.-invested capital	3,100			150	3,250
O.E.-retained earnings	2,630	1,690		(750)	3,570
Liabilities & owners' equity	$13,210	$1,990		($350)	$14,850

Figure 4-1: *Summary of changes in assets, liabilities, and owners' equity during the year*

Figure 4-1 is *not* a balance sheet. The balance sheet for this business is presented later in the chapter (see Figure 4-2). Businesses do not report a summary of changes in assets, liabilities, and owners' equity such as the one shown in Figure 4-1 (although such a summary would be helpful to users of financial reports).

The purpose of Figure 4-1 is to demonstrate how the three major types of transactions during the year change the business's assets, liabilities, and owners' equity accounts during the year.

The 2020 income statement of the business in the example is shown in Figure 3-1 in Chapter 3. You may want to flip to that financial statement. On sales revenue of $26 million, the business earned $1.69 million bottom-line profit (net income) for the year. The business's sales and expense transactions during the year plus the allied transactions connected with sales and expenses cause the changes shown in the operating activities column in Figure 4-1. You can see in Figure 4-1 that the $1.69 million net income has increased the business's owners' equity-retained earnings by the same amount.

The operating activities column in Figure 4-1 is worth lingering over for a few moments because it shows the financial outcomes of making profit. Most people see a profit number, such as the $1.69 million in this example, and stop thinking any further about the financial outcomes of making the profit. This is like going to a movie because you like its title but don't know anything about the plot and characters. You probably noticed that the $1,515,000 increase in cash in this column differs from the $1,690,000 net income figure for the year. The cash effect of making profit (which includes the allied transactions connected with sales and expenses) is almost always different than the net income amount for the year. Chapter 5 on cash flows explains this difference.

The summary of changes presented in Figure 4-1 gives a sense of the balance sheet in motion, or how the business got from the start of the year to the end of the year. It's important to have a good sense of how transactions propel the balance sheet. A summary of balance sheet changes, such as the one shown in Figure 4-1, can be helpful to business managers who plan and control changes in the business's assets and liabilities. They need a clear understanding of how the three basic types of transactions change assets and liabilities. Also, Figure 4-1 provides a useful platform for the statement of cash flows, which we explain in Chapter 5.

A Proper Balance Sheet

Figure 4-2 presents a two-year comparative balance sheet for the business example introduced in Chapter 3. The balance sheet is at the close of business, December 31, 2019 and 2020. In most cases financial statements are not completed and released until a few weeks after the balance sheet date. Therefore, by the time you would read this financial statement it's already out of date, because the business has continued to engage in transactions after December 31, 2020. (Managers of a business get internal financial statements much sooner.) When substantial changes have occurred in the interim, a business should disclose these developments in its financial report.

Typical Product Business, Inc.
Statement of Financial Position
at December 31, 2019 and 2020
(Dollar amounts in thousands)

Assets	2019	2020
Cash	$2,275	$2,165
Accounts receivable	2,150	2,600
Inventory	2,725	3,450
Prepaid expenses	525	600
Current assets	7,675	8,815
Property, plant, and equipment	11,175	12,450
Accumulated depreciation	(5,640)	(6,415)
Net of depreciation	5,535	6,035
Total assets	$13,210	$14,850

Liabilities and Owners' Equity	2019	2020
Accounts payable	$640	$765
Accrued expenses payable	750	900
Income tax payable	90	115
Short-term notes payable	2,150	2,250
Current liabilities	3,630	4,030
Long-term notes payable	3,850	4,000
Owners' equity:		
Invested capital	3,100	3,250
Retained earnings	2,630	3,570
Total owners' equity	5,730	6,820
Total liabilities and owners' equity	$13,210	$14,850

Figure 4-2: *The balance sheets of a business at the end of its two most recent years*

When a business does not release its annual financial report within a few weeks after the close of its fiscal year, you should be alarmed. The reasons for such a delay are all bad. One reason might be that the business's accounting system is not functioning well and the controller (chief accounting officer) has to do a lot of work at year-end to get the accounts up-to-date and accurate for preparing the financial statements. Another reason might be that the business is facing serious problems and can't decide on how to account for the problems. Perhaps a business may be delaying the reporting of bad news. Or the business may have a serious dispute with its independent auditor that has not been resolved.

In reading through a balance sheet such as the one shown in Figure 4-2, you may notice that it doesn't have a punch line like the income statement does. The income statement's punch line is the net income line. (Earnings per share is also important for public corporations.) You can't look at just one item on the balance sheet, murmur an appreciative "ah-ha," and rush home to watch the game. You have to read the entire thing (sigh) and make comparisons among the items.

Notice in Figure 4-2 that the beginning and ending balances in the assets, liabilities, and owners' equity accounts are the same as in Figure 4-1. The balance sheet in Figure 4-2 discloses the original cost of the company's fixed assets and the accumulated depreciation recorded over the years since acquisition of the assets, which is standard practice. (Figure 4-1 presents only the *net* book value of its fixed assets, which equals original cost minus accumulated depreciation.)

The financial statement in Figure 4-2 is called a *classified balance sheet* because certain accounts are grouped into classes (groups). Although the accounts in the class are different, they have common characteristics. Two such classes are *current assets* and *current liabilities*. Note that subtotals are provided for each class. The reasons for reporting these classes of accounts are discussed in the later section "Liquidity and solvency." The total amount of assets and the total amount of liabilities plus owners' equity are given at the bottom of the columns for each year.

The balance sheet of a service business and a product business look pretty much the same — except a service business doesn't report an inventory of products held for sale. If it sells on credit, a service business has an accounts receivable asset, just like a product company that sells on credit. The size of its total assets relative to annual sales revenue for a service business varies greatly from industry to industry, depending on whether or not the service industry is *capital intensive*. Some service businesses, such as airlines, utility companies, hospitals, and hotel chains, need to make heavy investments in long-term operating assets. Other service businesses do not.

The balance sheet is unlike the income and cash flow statements, which report flows over a period of time (such as sales revenue that is the cumulative amount of all sales during the period). The balance sheet presents the *balances* (amounts) of a company's assets, liabilities, and owners' equity at an instant in time. Note the two quite different meanings of the term *balance:*

- As used in *balance sheet,* the term *balance* refers to the equality of the two opposing sides of a business — total assets on the one side and total liabilities and owners' equity on the other side, like a scale with equal weights on both sides.

- In contrast, the *balance* of an account (asset, liability, owners' equity, revenue, and expense) refers to the amount in the account after recording increases and decreases in the account — the net amount after all additions and subtractions have been entered.

Usually, the meaning of the term is clear in context.

An accountant can prepare a balance sheet any time a manager wants to know how things stand financially. Some businesses — particularly financial institutions such as banks, mutual funds, and securities brokers — need balance sheets at the end of each day, to track their day-to-day financial situation. For most businesses, however, balance sheets are prepared only at the end of each month, quarter, and year. A balance sheet is always prepared at the close of business on the last day of the profit period. In other words, the balance sheet should be in sync with the income statement.

Balance sheets in the real world

The statement of financial position, or balance sheet, shown in Figure 4-2 is about as lean and mean as you'll ever read. In the real world, many businesses are fat and complex. Also, note that Figure 4-2 shows the content and format for an *external* balance sheet, which means a balance sheet included in a financial report released outside a business to its owners and creditors. Balance sheets that stay within a business can be quite different.

Internal balance sheets

For internal reporting of financial condition to managers, balance sheets include much more detail, either in the body of the financial statement itself or, more likely, in supporting schedules. For example, Figure 4-2 shows just one cash account, but the chief financial officer of a business needs to know the balances on deposit in each of the business's chequing accounts.

As another example, the balance sheet in Figure 4-2 includes just one total amount for accounts receivable, but managers need details on which customers owe money and whether any major amounts are past due. Greater detail allows for better control, analysis, and decision making. Internal balance sheets and their supporting schedules should provide all the detail that managers need to make good business decisions.

External balance sheets

Balance sheets presented in external financial reports (which go out to investors and lenders) do not include much more detail than the balance sheet in Figure 4-2.

CSIS (Canadian Security Intelligence Service) and the RCMP do not vet balance sheets to keep secrets from being disclosed that would harm national security. The term *classified,* when applied to a balance sheet, does not mean restricted or top secret; rather, the term means that assets and liabilities are sorted into basic classes, or groups, for external reporting. However, external balance sheets must classify (or group together) short-term assets and liabilities, property, plant, and equipment, intangible assets, long-term investments, and goodwill, so these sheets are referred to as classified balance sheets. Certain assets and liabilities are classified into *current* categories mainly to help readers of a balance sheet more easily compare current assets with current liabilities for the purpose of judging the short-term liquidity and solvency of a business. Generally, an accountant classifies an asset as current if the business expects to use it up in operations in the next 12 months. A liability is current if the business expects to pay it in the next 12 months.

Liquidity and solvency

Liquidity refers to the business's capability to pay its current liabilities when they are due. *Solvency*, on the other hand, refers to the business's capability to pay all of its liabilities on time. Delays in paying liabilities on time can cause serious problems for a business. In extreme cases, a business can be thrown into *involuntary bankruptcy*. Even the threat of bankruptcy can cause serious disruptions in the normal operations of a business, and profit performance is bound to suffer. If current liabilities become too high relative to current assets — which constitute the first line of defence for paying current liabilities — managers should move quickly to resolve the problem. A perceived shortage of current assets relative to current liabilities could ring alarm bells in the minds of the company's creditors and owners.

Therefore, note in Figure 4-2 the following groupings (dollar amounts refer to year-end 2020):

- The first four asset accounts (cash, accounts receivable, inventory, and prepaid expenses) are added to give the $8,815,000 subtotal for *current assets.*

- The first four liability accounts (accounts payable, accrued expenses payable, income tax payable, and short-term notes payable) are added to give the $4.03 million subtotal for *current liabilities.*

- The total interest-bearing debt of the business is separated between $2.25 million in *short-term* notes payable and $4 million in *long-term* notes payable. (In Figure 4-1, only one total amount for all interest-bearing debt is given, which is $6.25 million.)

The following sections offer more detail about current assets and liabilities.

Current (short-term) assets

Short-term, or *current,* assets are as follows:

- Cash
- Marketable securities that can be converted into cash
- Assets converted into cash or used in operations within one operating cycle

The *operating cycle* refers to the repetitive process of putting cash into inventory, holding products in inventory until they are sold, selling products on credit (which generates accounts receivable), and collecting the receivables in cash. In other words, the operating cycle is the "from cash through inventory and accounts receivable and back to cash" sequence. The operating cycles of businesses vary from a few weeks to several months, depending on how long inventory is held before being sold and how long it takes to collect cash from sales made on credit.

Current (short-term) liabilities

Short-term, or *current,* liabilities include non-interest-bearing liabilities that arise from the business's operating (sales and expense) activities. A typical business keeps many accounts for these liabilities — a separate account for each vendor, for instance. In an external balance sheet you usually find only three or four operating liabilities, and they are not labelled as non-interest-bearing. It is assumed that the reader knows that these operating liabilities don't bear interest (unless the liability is seriously overdue and the creditor has started charging interest because of the delay in paying the liability).

The balance sheet example shown in Figure 4-2 discloses three operating liabilities: accounts payable, accrued expenses payable, and income tax payable. Be warned that the terminology for these short-term operating liabilities varies from business to business.

In addition to operating liabilities, interest-bearing notes payable that have maturity dates one year or less from the balance sheet date are included in the current liabilities section. The current liabilities section may also include certain other liabilities that must be paid in the short run (which are too varied and technical to discuss here).

Current ratio

The sources of cash for paying current liabilities are the company's current assets. That is, current assets are the first source of money to pay current liabilities when these liabilities come due. Keep in mind that current assets consist of cash and assets that will be converted into cash in the short run. To size up current assets against total current liabilities, the *current ratio* is calculated. Using information from the company's balance sheet (refer to Figure 4-2), you calculate its year-end 2020 current ratio as follows:

$8,815,000 current assets ÷ $4,030,000 current liabilities = 2.2 current ratio

Generally, businesses do not provide their current ratio on the face of their balance sheets or in the notes to their financial statements — they leave it to the reader to calculate this number. On the other hand, many businesses present a financial highlights section in their financial report, which often includes the current ratio.

Quick ratio

The *quick ratio* is more restrictive. Only cash and assets that can be quickly converted into cash are included, which excludes inventory and prepaid expenses. The business in this example doesn't have any short-term marketable investments that could be sold on a moment's notice, so only cash and accounts receivable are included for the ratio. You compute the quick ratio as follows (see Figure 4-2):

$4,765,000 quick assets ÷ $4,030,000 current liabilities = 1.2 quick ratio

Folklore has it that a company's current ratio should be at least 2.0. However, business managers know that an acceptable current ratio depends a great deal on general practices in the industry for short-term borrowing. Some businesses do well with a current ratio less than 2.0, so take the 2.0 benchmark with a grain of salt. Retailers with high inventory turnover such as Loblaw or Wal-Mart have low current ratios. A lower current ratio does not necessarily mean that the business won't be able to pay its short-term (current) liabilities on time.

Assets and liabilities

When you first read the balance sheet in Figure 4-2, did you wonder about the size of the company's assets, liabilities, and owners' equities? Did you ask, "Are the balance sheet accounts about the right size?" The balances in a company's balance sheet accounts should be compared with the sales revenue size of the business. The amount of assets needed to carry on the profit-making transactions of a business depend mainly on the size of its annual revenue. And the sizes of its assets, in turn, largely determine the sizes of its liabilities — which, in turn, determines the size of its owners' equity accounts (although the ratio of liabilities and owners' equity depends on other factors as well).

Although the business example used in this chapter is hypothetical, random numbers weren't used. The example uses a modest-sized business that has $26 million in annual sales revenue. The other numbers in its income statement and balance sheet are realistic relative to each other. It's assumed that the business earns 45 percent gross margin ($11.7 million gross margin ÷ $26 million sales revenue = 45 percent), which means its cost of goods sold expense is 55 percent of sales revenue. The sizes of particular assets and liabilities compared with their relevant income statement numbers vary from industry to industry, and even from business to business in the same industry.

The managers of a business can estimate what the size of each asset and liability should be based on its history and operating policies, which provide useful *control benchmarks* against which the actual balances of the assets and liabilities are compared to highlight any serious deviations. In other words, assets (and liabilities, too) can be too high or too low relative to the sales revenue and expenses that drive them, and these deviations can cause problems that managers should try to correct.

For example, based on the credit terms extended to its customers and the company's policies regarding how aggressively it acts in collecting past-due receivables, a manager determines the range for the proper, or within-the-boundaries, balance of accounts receivable. This figure is the control benchmark. If the actual balance is reasonably close to this control benchmark, accounts receivable is under control. If not, the manager should investigate why accounts receivable is smaller or larger than it should be.

The following sections discuss the relative sizes of the assets and liabilities in the balance sheet that result from sales and expenses (for the fiscal year 2020). The sales and expenses are the *drivers*, or causes, of the assets and liabilities. If a business earned profit simply by investing in stocks and bonds, it would not need all the various assets and liabilities explained in this chapter. Such a business — a mutual fund, for example — would have just one income-producing asset: investments in securities. This chapter focuses on merchandising businesses that sell products on credit.

Sales revenue and accounts receivable

In Figure 4-3, annual sales revenue for the year 2020 is $26 million. The average accounts receivable for 2020 is $2.375 million. The average customer's credit period is roughly 33 days: 365 days in the year times the 10.9 percent ratio of average accounts receivable balance to annual sales revenue. Of course, some customers' balances are past 33 days, and some are quite new; you want to focus on the average. The key question is whether a customer credit period averaging 33 days is reasonable.

Suppose that the business offers all customers a 30-day credit period, which is fairly common in business-to-business selling (although not for a retailer selling to individual consumers). The relatively small deviation of about 3 days (33 days average credit period versus 30 days normal credit terms) probably is not a significant cause for concern. But suppose that the average accounts receivable had been $3.9 million, which is 15 percent of annual sales, or about a 55-day average credit period. Such an abnormally high balance should raise a red flag; the responsible manager should look into the reasons for the abnormally high accounts receivable balance. Perhaps several customers are seriously late in paying and should not be extended new credit until they pay up. (The increase in receivables could also be attributed to the seasonal nature of sales — for instance, a Christmas store might not see much income in July, but could do well in November — or to a disproportionately large sale close to the date the receivables were tabulated.)

Income Statement

Sales revenue	$26,000,000
Cost of goods sold expense	14,300,000
Gross margin	11,700,000
Depreciation expense	775,000
Selling, general, and administrative expenses	7,925,000
Operating earnings	3,000,000
Interest expense	400,000
Earnings before income tax	2,600,000
Income tax expense	910,000
Net income	$1,690,000

Non-Cash Assets

Accounts receivable	$2,600,000
Inventory	3,450,000
Prepaid expenses	600,000
Fixed assets, at original cost	12,450,000
Accumulated depreciation	(6,415,000)

Liabilities

Accounts payable	765,000
Accrued expenses payable	900,000
Income tax payable	115,000

Owners' Equity

Retained earnings	

Figure 4-3: *The connections between sales revenue and expenses and the non-cash assets and liabilities driven by these profit-making activities*

Cost of goods sold expense and inventory

In Figure 4-3, the cost of goods sold expense for the year 2020 is $14.3 million. The average inventory for 2020 is $3.088 million, or about 22 percent. In rough terms, the average product's inventory holding period is 80 days — 365 days in the year times the 22 percent ratio of ending inventory to annual cost of goods sold. Of course, some products may remain in inventory longer than the 80-day average, and some products may sell in a much shorter period than 80 days. You need to focus on the overall average. Is an 80-day average inventory holding period reasonable?

The "correct" average inventory holding period varies from industry to industry. In some industries, especially heavy equipment manufacturing, the inventory holding period is three months or longer. The opposite is true for high-volume retailers, such as retail supermarkets, which depend on getting products off the shelves as quickly as possible. The 80-day average holding period in the example is reasonable for many businesses but would be too high for some businesses.

The managers should know what the company's average inventory holding period should be — they should know the control benchmark for the inventory holding period. If inventory is much above this control benchmark, managers should take prompt action to get inventory back in line (which is easier said than done, of course). If inventory is at abnormally low levels, this should be investigated as well. Perhaps some products are out of stock and should be immediately restocked to avoid lost sales.

Fixed assets and depreciation expense

As Chapter 3 explains, depreciation is a relatively unique expense. Depreciation is like other expenses in that all expenses are deducted from sales revenue to determine profit. Other than this, however, depreciation is different from other expenses. When a business buys or builds a long-term operating asset, the cash outlay for the asset is recorded in a fixed asset account. The cost of a fixed asset is spread out, or allocated, over its expected useful life to the business. The depreciation expense recorded in the period does not require any further cash outlay during the period. (The cash outlay occurred when the fixed asset was acquired.) Rather, depreciation expense for the period is that portion of the total cost of a business's fixed assets that is allocated to the period to record the cost of using the assets during the period. Depreciation depends on which method is used to allocate the cost of fixed assets over their estimated useful lives.

The higher the total cost of its fixed assets (called *property, plant, and equipment* in a formal balance sheet), the higher a business's depreciation expense. However, no standard ratio of depreciation expense to the cost of fixed assets exists. The annual depreciation expense of a business seldom is more than 10 to 15 percent of the original cost of its fixed assets. Either the depreciation expense for the year is reported as a separate expense in the income statement (as in Figure 4-3), or the amount is disclosed in a note.

Because depreciation is based on the gradual charging off, or writing-down, of the cost of a fixed asset, the balance sheet reports not one but two numbers: the original (historical) cost of its fixed assets and the *accumulated depreciation* amount (the total amount of depreciation that has been charged to expense from the time of acquiring the fixed assets to the current balance sheet date). The purpose isn't to confuse you by giving you even more numbers to deal with. Seeing both numbers gives you an idea of how old the fixed assets are and also tells you how much these fixed assets originally cost and when they will likely need replacing. By the way, GAAP rules require the disclosure of these amounts.

In the example in this chapter, the business has, over several years, invested $12,450,000 in its fixed assets (that it still owns and uses), and it has recorded total depreciation of $6,415,000 through the end of the most recent fiscal year, December 31,

2020. (Refer to the balance sheet presented in Figure 4-2.) The business recorded $775,000 depreciation expense in its most recent year. (Refer to the income statement in Figure 4-3.)

You can tell that the company's collection of fixed assets includes some old assets because the company has recorded $6,415,000 total depreciation since assets were bought — a fairly sizable percentage of original cost (more than half). But many businesses use accelerated depreciation methods that pile up a lot of the depreciation expense in the early years and less in the back years, so estimating the average age of the company's assets is hard. A business could discuss the actual ages of its fixed assets in the notes to its financial statements, but hardly any businesses disclose this information — although they do identify which depreciation methods they are using.

SG&A expenses and their three balance sheet accounts

Sales, general, and administrative (SG&A) expenses connect with three balance sheet accounts: prepaid expenses, accounts payable, and accrued expenses payable. The broad SG&A expense category includes many different types of expenses in making sales and operating the business. (Separate expense accounts are maintained for specific expenses; depending on the business's size and the needs of its various managers, hundreds or thousands of specific expense accounts are established.)

For bookkeeping convenience, a business records many expenses when the expense is paid. For example, wage and salary expenses are recorded on payday. However, this "record as you pay" method does not work for many expenses. For instance, insurance and office supplies costs are *prepaid*, and then released to expense gradually over time. The cost is initially put in the *prepaid expenses* asset account. (Yes, "prepaid expenses" doesn't sound like an asset account, but it is.) Other expenses are not paid until weeks after the expenses are recorded. The amounts owed for these unpaid expenses are recorded in an *accounts payable* or in an *accrued expenses payable* liability account.

This chapter doesn't go through all the details of how we came up with the year-end balances in prepaid expenses, accounts payable, and accrued expenses payable. For more details, you may want to take a look at Chapter 3. Keep in mind that the accounting objective is to match expenses with sales revenue for the year, and only in this way can the amount of profit be measured for the year. So expenses recorded for the year should be the correct amounts, regardless of when they're paid.

Intangible assets, goodwill, and amortization expense

Although this chapter's business example does not include intangible assets, goodwill, and amortization expense, many businesses invest in intangible assets. *Intangible* means without physical existence, in contrast to buildings, vehicles, and computers. For example:

- A business might purchase the customer list of another company that is going out of business.

- A business might buy patent rights from the inventor of a new product or process.

- A business might buy another business lock, stock, and barrel and pay more than the total of the individual assets of the company being bought are worth — even after adjusting the particular assets to their current values. The extra amount is for *goodwill*, which may consist of a trained and efficient workforce, an established product with a reputation for high quality, or a valuable location.

Most intangible assets used by a business are purchased and recorded by that business. To be recognized in the accounts, goodwill must have been purchased. A business must expend cash, take on debt, or issue owners' equity shares for an intangible asset to record the asset on its books. Building up a good reputation with customers or establishing a well-known brand is not recorded as goodwill. You can imagine the value of Coca-Cola's brand name, but this "asset" is not recorded on the company's books. (However, Coca-Cola protects its brand name with all the legal means at its disposal to maintain the competitive advantage it enjoys from name recognition.)

The cost of an intangible asset is put in the appropriate asset account, just like the cost of a tangible asset is recorded in a fixed asset account. And, like a fixed asset account (with the exception of land), the cost of an intangible asset that has a limited useful economic life is allocated over its estimated useful life. (Note that certain intangible assets are viewed as having more or less perpetual useful lives.) The allocation of the cost of an intangible asset over its estimated economic life is called *amortization*. Amortization expense is similar to depreciation expense.

For intangible assets and goodwill with unlimited useful lives, instead of recording amortization, accounting guidelines dictate that these assets be tested for any impairment in their capability to help produce income. Should they be determined to be impaired, an impairment loss is recorded. Impairment losses on the income statement can be huge. Because this chapter's business example does not include any intangible assets, no amortization expense or impairment loss applies.

Debt and interest expense

Look at the balance sheet shown in Figure 4-2. Note that the sum of this business's short-term (current) and long-term notes payable at year-end 2020 is $6.25 million. The average of this debt in 2020 is $61,250. From its income statement in Figure 4-3, you see that its interest expense for the year was $400,000. Based on the average amount of debt, the annual interest rate is about 6.5 percent. (The business may have had more or less borrowed at certain times during the year, of course, and the actual interest rate depends on the debt levels from month to month.)

For most businesses, a small part of their total annual interest is unpaid at year-end; the unpaid part is recorded to bring interest expense up to the correct total amount for the year. In Figure 4-3, the accrued amount of interest is included in the *accrued expenses payable* liability account. In most balance sheets you don't find accrued interest payable on a separate line; rather, it's included in the accrued expenses payable liability account. However, if unpaid interest at year-end happens to be a rather large amount, or if the business is seriously behind in paying interest on its debt, it should report the accrued interest payable as a separate liability.

Income tax expense and income tax payable

In Figure 4-3, earnings before income tax — after deducting interest and all other expenses from sales revenue — is $2.6 million. The actual taxable income of the business for the year probably is different than this amount because of the many complexities in the income tax law. The example uses a realistic 35 percent tax rate, so the income tax expense is $910,000 of the pre-tax income of $2.6 million.

A large part of the income tax amount for the year must be paid to the CRA in monthly instalments before the end of the year. But a small part is usually still owed at the end of the year. The unpaid part is recorded in the *income tax payable* liability account, as you see in Figure 4-3. In the example, the unpaid part is $115,000 of the total $910,000 income tax for the year, but this doesn't mean that this ratio is typical. Generally, the unpaid income tax at the end of the year is fairly small, but just how small depends on several technical factors.

Net income and cash dividends (if any)

A business may have other sources of income during the year, such as interest income on investments. In this example, however, the business has only sales revenue, which is gross income from the sale of products and services. All expenses — starting with cost of goods sold down to and including income tax — are deducted from sales revenue to arrive at the last, or bottom, line of the income statement. The preferred term for bottom-line profit is *net income,* as you see in Figure 4-3.

The $1.69 million net income for the year increases the owners' equity account *retained earnings* by the same amount, which is indicated by the line of connection from net income to retained earnings in Figure 4-3. The $1.69 million profit (yes, here's the use of the term *profit* instead of *net income*) either stays in the business or some of it is paid out and divided among the business's owners. This business paid out cash distributions from profit during the year, and the total of these cash payments to its owners (shareholders) is recorded as a decrease in retained earnings.

As discussed in Chapter 3, you have to look at the statement of retained earnings if you are a private enterprise, or the statement of changes in equity if you are a public corporation. You can't tell from the income statement or the balance sheet the amount of cash dividends. You could also look in the statement of cash flows for this information (which is explained in Chapter 5).

The Financing of a Business

To run a business, you need financial backing, otherwise known as *capital.* In broad overview, a business raises capital needed for its assets by buying things on credit, waiting to pay some expenses, borrowing money, getting owners to invest money in the business, and making profit that is retained in the business. Borrowed money is known as *debt;* capital invested in the business by its owners and retained profits are the two sources of *owners' equity.*

How did the business whose balance sheet is shown in Figure 4-2 finance its assets? Its total assets are $14.85 million at year-end 2020. The company's profit-making activities generated three liabilities — accounts payable, accrued expenses payable, and income tax payable — and in total these three liabilities provided $1.78 million of the business's total assets. Debt provided $6.25 million, and the two sources of owners' equity provided the other $6.82 million. All three sources add up to $14.85 million, which equals total assets, of course. Otherwise, its books would be out of balance, which is a definite no-no.

Accounts payable, accrued expenses payable, and income tax payable are short-term, non-interest-bearing liabilities that are sometimes called *spontaneous liabilities* because they arise directly from a business's expense activities. They aren't the result of borrowing money but rather are the result of buying things on credit or delaying payment of certain expenses.

Avoiding these three liabilities in running a business is hard; they are generated naturally in the process of carrying on operations. In contrast, the mix of debt (interest-bearing liabilities) and equity (invested owners' capital and retained earnings) requires careful thought and high-level decisions by a business. No natural or automatic answer to the debt-versus-equity question exists. The business in the example has a large amount of debt relative to its owners' equity, which would make many business owners uncomfortable.

 Debt is both good and bad, and in extreme situations it can get ugly. The advantages of debt follow:

- Most businesses can't raise all the capital they need from owners' equity sources, and debt offers another source of capital (though, of course, many lenders are willing to provide only part of the capital that a business needs).

- Interest expense is tax deductible, so the real cost of interest is lower than the amount of interest paid.

- Interest rates charged by lenders are lower than rates of return expected by owners. Owners expect a higher rate of return because they're taking a greater risk with their money — the business is not required to pay them back the same way that it's required to pay back a lender. For example, a business may pay 6 percent annual interest on its debt and be expected to earn a 12 percent annual rate of return on its owners' equity.

And following are the disadvantages of debt:

- A business must pay the agreed-upon rate of interest for the period even if it suffers a loss for the period or earns a lower rate of return on its assets.

- A business must be ready to pay back the debt on the specified due date, which can cause some pressure on the business to come up with the money on time. (Of course, a business may be able to *roll over*, or renew, its debt, meaning that it replaces its old debt with an equivalent amount of new debt, but the lender has the right to demand that the old debt be paid and not rolled over.)

If a business defaults on its debt contract — it doesn't pay the interest on time or doesn't pay back the debt on the due date — it faces some major unpleasantness. In extreme cases, a lender can force it to shut down and liquidate its assets (that is, sell off everything it owns for cash) to pay off the debt and unpaid interest. Just as you can lose your home if you don't pay your home mortgage, a business can be forced into involuntary bankruptcy if it doesn't pay its debts. A lender may allow the business to try to work out its financial crisis through receivership or bankruptcy procedures, but bankruptcy is a nasty affair that invariably causes many problems and can cripple or terminate a business.

Costs and Other Balance Sheet Values

The values for assets reported in a balance sheet can be a source of confusion for both business managers and investors, who tend to put all dollar amounts on the same value basis. In their minds, a dollar is a dollar, whether it's in accounts receivable, inventory, fixed assets, accounts payable, or retained earnings. But some dollars are much older than other dollars.

The dollar amounts reported in a balance sheet are the result of the transactions recorded in the assets, liabilities, and owners' equity accounts. Some transactions from years ago may still have life in the present balances of certain assets. For example, business-owned land that is reported in the balance sheet goes back to the transaction for the purchase of the land, which could be 20 or 30 years ago. The balance in the land asset is standing in the same asset column, for example, as the balance in the accounts receivable asset, which likely is only one or two months old.

Book values (sometimes referred to as *carrying amounts*) are the amounts recorded in the accounting process and reported in financial statements. Don't assume that the book values reported in a balance sheet necessarily equal the current market values. Book values are based on the accounting methods used by a business. Generally speaking, the amounts reported for cash, accounts receivable, and liabilities are equal to or are close to their current market or settlement values.

For example, accounts receivable will be turned into cash for the amount recorded on the balance sheet, and liabilities will be paid off at the amounts reported in the balance sheet. The book values of inventory and fixed assets, as well as any other assets in which the business invested some time ago, are most likely lower than current market values.

Also, keep in mind that a business may have unrecorded assets. These off-balance-sheet assets include a well-known reputation for quality products and excellent service, secret formulas (think Coca-Cola), patents that are the result of its research and development over the years, and a better trained workforce than its competitors. The business did not purchase these intangible assets from outside sources but rather accumulated them over the years through its own efforts. These assets, though not reported in the balance sheet, should show up in better-than-average profit performance in the business's income statement.

Different businesses select different accounting methods to determine their cost of inventory and how much of each of their fixed assets' costs are allocated to depreciation expense each year. A business is free to use conservative accounting methods — with the result that its inventory cost value and the undepreciated cost of its fixed assets may be considerably lower than the current values of these assets.

A business may use accounting methods that have the effect of recording higher profit and higher asset values than would exist under more conservative accounting methods. Even so, the current values of its inventory and fixed assets may be quite a bit higher than the recorded costs of these assets, in particular for buildings, land, heavy machinery, and equipment. For example, the aircraft fleet of Air Canada, as reported in its balance sheet, is hundreds of millions of dollars less than the current cost it would have to pay to replace the planes. Complicating matters is the fact that many of its older planes are not being produced anymore, and Air Canada would replace the older planes with newer models.

Private businesses in Canada using Accounting Standards for Private Enterprises (ASPE) aren't permitted to write up the book values of their assets to current market or replacement values. On the other hand, investments in marketable securities have to be written up, or down, for all companies in Canada. Investment property or rental real estate may be revalued to fair value when following IFRS. Some accountants believe that although recording market values has intuitive appeal, a market-to-market valuation model is not practical or appropriate for businesses that sell products and services. They believe that these businesses do not stand ready to sell their assets (other than inventory); they need their assets for operating the business into the future. At the end of their useful lives, assets are sold for their disposable or residual values (or traded in for new assets).

Don't think that the market value of a business is simply equal to its owners' equity reported in its most recent balance sheet. Putting a value on a business depends on several factors in addition to the latest balance sheet of the business.

5

Reporting Cash Flows

Suppose that a business's cash balance decreases $110,000 during the year. You see this decrease in the company's balance sheets for the years ending December 31, 2019 and 2020. The business started the year with $2,275,000 cash and ended the year with $2,165,000 (as in the business example used in Chapters 3 and 4). What does the balance sheet tell you about the reasons for the cash decrease? Well, not a whole lot. Answering such a question is not the nature or purpose of a balance sheet.

One possibility is that the business suffered a large loss in 2020 that caused a drain on cash. You can look at its 2020 income statement to find out whether the business had a loss or made a profit, but this financial statement does *not* report the cash flow effect from the loss or profit. Another possibility for the cash decrease is that the business paid down its debt. Or perhaps the company made large investments in new machines and equipment during the year. Where do you look for such information? Answering this question is the main purpose of this chapter, which introduces the third key financial statement: the statement of cash flows.

The *statement of cash flows* has two purposes: It explains why cash flow from profit differs from bottom-line profit, and it summarizes the investing and financing activities of the business during the period. This may seem like an odd mix to put into one financial statement, but it makes sense. Earning profit (net income) generates net cash inflow (at least, it should normally). Making profit is a primary source of cash to a business. The investing and financing transactions of a business hinge on its cash flow from profit. All sources and uses of cash hang together and should be managed in an integrated manner.

The Basics of the Statement of Cash Flows

The income statement (see Chapter 3) has a natural structure: Revenue – Expenses = Profit (Net Income)

So does the balance sheet (see Chapter 4): Assets = Liabilities + Owners' Equity

The statement of cash flows doesn't have an obvious natural structure, so the accounting rule-making body had to decide on the basic format for the statement. It settled on the following structure:

$$\pm \text{ Cash Flow from Operating Activities}$$
$$\pm \text{ Cash Flow from Investing Activities}$$
$$\pm \text{ Cash Flow from Financing Activities}$$
$$= \text{Cash Increase or Decrease during Period}$$
$$+ \text{ Beginning Cash Balance}$$
$$= \text{ Ending Cash Balance}$$

The plus/minus sign means that the cash flow could be positive or negative. Generally, the cash flow from the investing activities of product businesses is negative, which means that the business spent more on new investments in long-term assets than cash received from disposals of previous investments. And generally, the cash flow from operating activities (profit-making activities) should be positive, unless the business spent more in cash than it took in during the year and drained cash out of the business.

The threefold classification of activities (transactions) reported in the statement of cash flows — operating, investing, and financing — are the same ones introduced in Chapter 4, which explains the balance sheet. The first figure in Chapter 4 (Figure 4-1) summarizes these transactions for the product company example that continues in this chapter.

The direct method

The statement of cash flows begins with the cash from making profit, or *cash flow from operating activities*, as accountants call it. *Operating activities* is the term accountants adopted for sales and expenses, which are the "operations" that a business carries out to earn profit. Furthermore, the term *operating activities* also includes the transactions coupled with sales and expenses. For example, making a sale on credit is an operating activity, and so is collecting the cash from the customer at a later time. Recording sales and expenses can be thought of as primary operating activities because they affect profit. Their associated transactions are secondary operating activities because they don't affect profit. However, they do affect cash flow, as explained in this chapter.

Figure 5-1 presents the statement of cash flows for the product business example introduced in Chapters 3 and 4. What you see in the first section of the statement of cash flows is called the *direct method* for reporting cash flow from operating activities. The dollar amounts are the cash flows connected with sales and expenses. For example, the business collected $25,550,000 from customers during the year, which is the direct result of making sales. The company paid $15,025,000 for the products it sells, some of which went toward increasing the inventory of products awaiting sale next period.

Typical Product Business, Inc.
Statement of Cash Flows
for Year Ended December 31, 2020
(Dollar amounts in thousands)

Cash Flows from Operating Activities

Collections from sales		$25,550
Payments for products	($15,025)	
Payments for selling, general, and administrative costs	(7,750)	
Payments for interest on debt	(375)	
Payments on income tax	(885)	(24,035)
Cash flow from operating activities		1,515

Cash Flows from Investing Activities

Expenditures on property, plant, and equipment		(1,275)

Cash Flows from Financing Activities

Short-term debt increase	100	
Long-term debt increase	150	
Capital stock issue	150	
Dividends paid shareholders	(750)	(350)
Decrease in cash during year		(110)
Beginning cash balance		2,275
Ending cash balance		$2,165

Figure 5-1: *The statement of cash flows — using the direct method for presenting cash flow from operating activities*

Note in Figure 5-1 that cash flow from operating activities for the year is $1,515,000, which is $175,000 less than the company's $1,690,000 net income for the year (refer to Figure 3-1). All of the main categories of sources and uses of cash are listed in the cash flows from operations using the direct format. For example, you can see the sheer size of the gross amount of total cash collected on sales. You can also see the proportion of that number against the size of the cash paid for the product that your business has sold. The amount of the difference between the cash collected and the cash paid for products represents the amount of gross profit of the business expressed in terms of cash instead of revenue and expenses.

Because the same business example in this chapter is used in Chapters 3 and 4, you may want to take a moment to review its 2020 income statement in Figure 3-1. And you may want to review Figure 4-1, which summarizes how the three types of activities changed its assets, liabilities, and owners' equity accounts during the year 2020.

The basic idea of the direct method is to present the sales revenue and expenses of the business on a cash basis, in contrast to the amounts reported in the income statement, which are on the accrual basis for recording revenue and expenses. *Accrual basis* accounting is real-time accounting that records transactions when economic events happen: Accountants record sales on credit when the sales take place, even though cash isn't collected from customers until sometime later. Cash payments for expenses occur before or after the expenses are recorded. *Cash basis* accounting is just what it says: Transactions aren't recorded until there's actual cash flow (in or out).

The revenue and expense cash flows you see in Figure 5-1 differ from the amounts you see in the accrual accounting basis income statement (refer to Figure 3-1). Herein lies a problem with the direct method. If you, a conscientious reader of the financial statements of a business, compare the revenues and expenses reported in the income statement with the cash flow amounts reported in the statement of cash flows, you may get confused. Which set of numbers is correct? Well, both are. The numbers in the income statement are the true numbers for measuring profit for the period. The numbers in the statement of cash flows are additional information for you to ponder.

The indirect method

A business can use the alternative method or format for reporting cash flow from operating activities. The alternative method starts with net income, and then makes adjustments to reconcile cash flow from operating activities with net income.

This alternative method is called the *indirect method,* which is shown in Figure 5-2. Although use of the direct method is strongly encouraged by the standard setters internationally and in Canada, in practice the indirect format is used more often. This may be because of the public's resistance to change, rather than an expression of a real preference.

The indirect method for reporting cash flow from operating activities focuses on the *changes* during the year in the assets and liabilities that are connected with sales and expenses. Find out more about these connections in Chapter 3. (You can also trace these changes back to Figure 4-1, which includes the start-of-year and end-of-year balances of the balance sheet accounts for the business example.)

Although obvious differences exist in the first section of the statement of cash flows between the two methods for reporting cash flow from operating activities, the other two sections of the statement — cash flow from investing activities and cash flow from financing activities — are the same. The level of detail disclosed in these two sections varies from business to business. For example, some companies report one amount for all capital expenditures (investments in new long-term operating assets), whereas others give a more detailed breakdown by type of asset.

Typical Product Business, Inc.
Statement of Cash Flows
for Year Ended December 31, 2020
(Dollar amounts in thousands)

Cash Flows from Operating Activities		
Net income		$1,690
Adjustments to net income for determining cash flow:		
Accounts receivable increase	($450)	
Inventory increase	(725)	
Prepaid expenses increase	(75)	
Depreciation expense	775	
Accounts payable increase	125	
Accrued expenses increase	150	
Income tax payable increase	25	(175)
Cash flow from operating activities		1,515
Cash Flows from Investing Activities		
Expenditures on property, plant, and equipment		(1,275)
Cash Flows from Financing Activities		
Short-term debt increase	100	
Long-term debt increase	150	
Shares issue	150	
Dividends paid shareholders	(750)	(350)
Decrease in cash during year		(110)
Beginning cash balance		2,275
Ending cash balance		$2,165

Figure 5-2: *The statement of cash flows — using the indirect method for presenting cash flow from operating activities*

The Difference between Cash Flow and Net Income

A positive cash flow from operating activities is the amount of cash generated by a business's profit-making operations during the year, exclusive of its other sources of cash during the year. Cash flow from operating activities indicates a business's capability to turn profit into available cash — cash in the bank that can be used for the needs of business. As you see in Figure 5-1 or Figure 5-2 (take your pick), the business in our example generated $1,515,000 cash from its profit-making activities in the year.

The business in the example experienced a strong growth year. Its accounts receivable and inventory increased by relatively large amounts. In fact, all its assets and liabilities intimately connected with sales and expenses increased; their ending balances are larger than their beginning balances (which are the amounts carried forward from the end of the preceding year). Of course, this may not always be the case in a growth situation; one or more assets and liabilities could decrease during the year. For flat, no-growth situations, having a mix of modest-sized increases and decreases is much more likely.

The following sections explain how the asset and liability changes affect cash flow from operating activities. As a business manager, keep a close watch on the changes in each of your assets and liabilities and understand the cash flow effects caused by these changes. Investors focus on the business's capability to generate a healthy cash flow from operating activities, so investors are also equally concerned about these changes. In some situations these changes can signal serious problems.

You may not be too interested in the details that are discussed in the following sections. With this in mind, at the start of each section you're presented with the punch line. If you want, you can just read this and move on. But the details are fascinating (well, at least to accountants).

Note: Instead of using the full phrase *cash flow from operating activities* every time, the following sections use the shorter term *cash flow*. All data for assets and liabilities are found in the two-year balance sheet of the business (refer to Figure 4-2).

Accounts receivable change

Punch Line: An increase in accounts receivable hurts cash flow; a decrease helps cash flow.

The accounts receivable asset shows how much money customers who bought products on credit still owe the business. This asset is a promise of cash that the business will receive. Basically, accounts receivable is the amount of uncollected sales revenue at the end of the period. Cash does not increase until the business collects money from its customers.

The business started the year with $2.15 million and ended the year with $2.6 million in accounts receivable. The beginning balance was collected during the year, but the ending balance had not been collected at the end of the year. Thus the *net* effect is a shortfall in cash inflow of $450,000. The key point is that you need to keep an eye on the increase or decrease in accounts receivable from the beginning of the period to the end of the period. Here's what to look for:

• If the amount of credit sales you made during the period is greater than what you collected from customers during the period, your accounts receivable *increased* over the period, and you need to *subtract* from net income that difference between start-of-period accounts receivable and end-of-period accounts receivable. In short, an increase in accounts receivable hurts cash flow by the amount of the increase.

• If the amount you collected from customers during the period is greater than the credit sales you made during the period, your accounts receivable *decreased* over the period, and you need to *add* to net income that difference between start-of-period accounts receivable and end-of-period accounts receivable. In short, a decrease in accounts receivable helps cash flow by the amount of the decrease. Reducing the amount that customers owe the business is good news from the cash flows perspective.

In the business example, accounts receivable increased $450,000. Cash collections from sales were $450,000 less than sales revenue. Ouch! The business increased its sales substantially over the last period, so you shouldn't be surprised that its accounts receivable increased. The higher sales revenue was good for profit but bad for cash flow.

 The lagging behind effect of cash flow is the price of growth — managers and investors need to understand this point. Increasing sales without increasing accounts receivable is a happy situation for cash flow, but in the real world you usually can't have one increase without the other.

Inventory change

Punch Line: An increase in inventory hurts cash flow; a decrease helps cash flow.

Inventory is usually the largest short-term, or *current*, asset of businesses that sell products. If the inventory account is greater at the end of the period than at the start of the period — because unit costs increased or because the quantity of products increased — the amount the business actually paid out in cash for inventory purchases (or for manufacturing products) is more than what the business recorded in the cost of goods sold expense for the period.

In the business example, inventory increased $725,000 from start-of-year to end-of-year. In other words, to support its higher sales levels in 2020, this business replaced the products that it sold during the year *and* increased its inventory by $725,000. The business had to come up with the cash to pay for this inventory increase. Basically, the business wrote cheques amounting to $725,000 more than its cost of goods sold expense for the period. This step-up in its inventory level was necessary to support the higher sales level, which increased profit even though cash flow took a hit. Having more cash tied up in inventory is bad news from a cash flow perspective.

Prepaid expenses change

Punch Line: An increase in prepaid expenses (an asset account) hurts cash flow; a decrease helps cash flow.

A change in the prepaid expenses asset account works the same way as a change in inventory and accounts receivable, although changes in prepaid expenses are usually much smaller than changes in those other two asset accounts.

The beginning balance of prepaid expenses is charged to expense this year, but the cash for this amount was actually paid out last year. This period (the year 2020 in the example), the business pays cash for next period's prepaid expenses, which affects this period's cash flow but doesn't affect net income until next period. In short, the $75,000 increase in prepaid expenses in this business example has a negative cash flow effect.

> As it grows, a business needs to increase its prepaid expenses for such things as fire insurance (premiums have to be paid in advance of the insurance coverage) and its inventory of office and data processing supplies. Increases in accounts receivable, inventory, and prepaid expenses are the cash flow price a business has to pay for growth. Rarely do you find a business that can increase its sales revenue without increasing these assets.

The depreciation factor

Punch Line: Recording depreciation expense decreases the book value of long-term operating (fixed) assets. No cash outlay occurs when recording depreciation expense. Each year the business converts in an indirect way part of the total cost invested in its fixed assets into cash. It recovers this amount through cash collections from sales. Thus, depreciation is a positive cash flow factor.

The original costs of fixed assets are recorded in a *property, plant, and equipment* type account. Depreciation is recorded in an *accumulated depreciation* account, which is a so-called *contra* account because its balance is deducted from the balance in the fixed asset account (see Figure 5-2). Recording depreciation increases the accumulated depreciation account, which decreases the book value of the fixed asset.

The amount of depreciation expense recorded in the period is a portion of the original cost of the business's fixed assets, most of which were bought and paid for years ago. (Chapters 3 and 4 explain more about depreciation.) Because the depreciation expense is not a cash outlay this period, the amount is added to net income to determine cash flow from operating activities (refer to Figure 5-2). Depreciation is just one adjustment factor to get from net income reported in the income statement to cash flow from operating activities reported in the statement of cash flows.

For measuring profit, depreciation is definitely an expense — no doubt about it. Buildings, machinery, equipment, tools, vehicles, computers, and office furniture are all on an irreversible journey to the junk heap (although buildings usually take a long time to get there). Fixed assets (except for land) have a limited, finite life of usefulness to a business; depreciation is the accounting method that allocates the total cost of fixed assets to each year of their use in helping the business generate sales revenue.

In the example, the business recorded $775,000 depreciation expense for the year. Instead of looking at depreciation as only an expense, consider the investment-recovery cycle of fixed assets. A business invests money in its fixed assets that are then used for several or many years. Over the life of a fixed asset, a business has to recover through sales revenue the cost invested in the fixed asset (ignoring any residual value at the end of its useful life). In a real sense, a business "sells" some of its fixed assets each period to its customers — it factors the cost of fixed assets into the sales prices that it charges its customers.

For example, when you go to a supermarket, a small slice of the price you pay for that litre of milk goes toward the cost of the building, the shelves, the refrigeration equipment, and so on. Each period, a business recoups part of the cost invested in its fixed assets. In the example, $775,000 of sales revenue went toward reimbursing the business for the use of its fixed assets during the year. In short, depreciation is a positive cash flow factor. The depreciation amount is embedded in sales revenue, and sales revenue generates cash flow.

The business in the example does not own any intangible assets and, thus, does not record any amortization expense. (Refer to Chapter 4 for an explanation of intangible assets and amortization.) If a business does own intangible assets, the amortization expense on these assets for the year is treated the same as depreciation is treated in the statement of cash flows. In other words, the recording of amortization expense does not require cash outlay in the year being charged with the expense. The cash outlay occurred in prior periods when the business invested in intangible assets.

Changes in operating liabilities

Punch Line: An increase in a short-term operating liability helps cash flow; a decrease hurts cash flow.

The business in the example, like almost all businesses, has three basic liabilities inextricably intertwined with its expenses:

- Accounts payable
- Accrued expenses payable
- Income tax payable

When the beginning balance of one of these liability accounts is the same as its ending balance (not too likely, of course), the business breaks even on cash flow for that account. When the end-of-period balance is higher than the start-of-period balance, the business did not pay out as much money as was recorded as an expense in the year.

In the example, the business disbursed $640,000 to pay off last year's accounts payable balance. (This $640,000 was the accounts payable balance at December 31, 2019, the end of the previous fiscal year.) Its cash this year decreased $640,000 because of these payments. But this year's ending balance sheet (at December 31, 2020) shows accounts payable of $765,000 that the business will not pay until the following year. This $765,000 amount was recorded to expense in the year 2020. So, the amount of expense was $125,000 more than the cash outlay for the year; or, in reverse, the cash outlay was $125,000 less than the expense. An increase in accounts payable benefits cash flow for the year. In other words, an increase in accounts payable has a positive cash flow effect. Increases in accrued expenses payable and income tax payable work the same way.

In short, liability increases are favourable to cash flow — in a sense, the business ran up more on credit than it paid off. Such an increase means that the business delayed paying cash for certain things until next year. So you need to add the increases in the three liabilities to net income to determine cash flow, as you see in the statement of cash flows (refer to Figure 5-2). The business avoided cash outlays to the extent of the increases in these three liabilities. In some cases, of course, the ending balance of an operating liability may be lower than its beginning balance, which means that the business paid out more cash than the corresponding expenses for the period. In this case, the decrease is a negative cash flow factor.

How to put the cash flow pieces together

Taking into account all the adjustments to net income, the bottom line (oops, you shouldn't use that term when referring to cash flow) is that the company's cash balance increased $1,515,000 from its operating activities during the year. The first section in the statement of cash flows (refer to Figure 5-2) shows the stepping stones from net income to the amount of cash flow from operating activities.

What do the figures in the first section of the cash flow statement (refer to Figure 5-2) reveal about this business over the past period? Recall that the business experienced sales growth during this period. The downside of sales growth is that assets and liabilities also grow — the business needs more inventory at the higher sales level and also has higher accounts receivable. The business's prepaid expenses and liabilities also increased, although not nearly as much as accounts receivable and inventory.

The growth of the business in 2020 over 2019 yielded higher profit but also caused a surge in its assets and liabilities — the result being that cash flow is $175,000 less than its net income. Still, the business had $1,515,000 cash at its disposal. What did the business do with this $1,515,000 of available cash? You have to look to the remainder of the cash flow statement to answer this important question.

The Rest of the Statement of Cash Flows

After you get past the first section of the statement of cash flows, the remainder is a breeze. Well, to be fair, you *could* encounter some rough seas in the remaining two sections. But, generally speaking, the information in these sections isn't too difficult to understand. The last two sections of the statement report on the other sources of cash to the business and the uses the business made of its cash during the year.

Investing activities

The second section of the statement of cash flows (refer to Figure 5-1 or 5-2) reports the investment actions that a business's managers took during the year. Investments, like tea leaves, serve as indicators regarding what the future may hold for the company. Major new investments are the sure signs of expanding or modernizing the production and distribution facilities and capacity of the business to make it more competitive. Major disposals of long-term assets and shedding off a major part of the business could be good news or bad news for the business, depending on many factors. Different investors may interpret this information differently, but all would agree that the information in this section of the cash flow statement is important.

Certain long-lived operating assets are required for doing business. For example, FedEx and UPS wouldn't be successful if they didn't have airplanes and trucks for delivering packages and computers for tracking deliveries. When these assets wear out, the business needs to replace them. Also, to remain competitive, a business may need to upgrade its equipment to take advantage of the latest technology or to provide for growth. These investments in long-lived, tangible, productive assets, which are called *property, plant, and equipment* or *fixed assets* for short, are critical to the business's future. In fact, these cash outlays are called *capital expenditures* to stress that capital is being invested for the long haul.

One of the first claims on cash flow from operating activities is for capital expenditures. Note that the business spent $1,275,000 on fixed assets, which are referred to more formally as *property, plant, and equipment* in the cash flow statement (to keep the terminology consistent with account titles used in the balance sheet — the term *fixed assets* is informal).

A typical statement of cash flows doesn't go into much detail regarding exactly what specific types of fixed assets the business purchased (or constructed): how many additional square feet of space the business acquired, how many new drill presses it bought, and so on. Some businesses do leave a clearer trail of their investments, though. For example, in the notes or elsewhere in their financial reports, airlines describe how many new aircraft of each kind were purchased to replace old equipment or to expand their fleets.

Usually, a business disposes of some of its fixed assets every year because they reached the end of their useful lives and will no longer be used. These fixed assets are sent to the junkyard, traded in on new fixed assets, or sold for relatively small amounts of money. The value of a fixed asset at the end of its useful life is called its *residual value.* The disposal proceeds from selling fixed assets are reported as a source of cash in the investing activities section of the statement of cash flows. Usually, these amounts are fairly small. Also, a business may sell off fixed assets because it's downsizing or abandoning a major segment of its business; these cash proceeds can be fairly large, particularly in the case of discontinued operations. Chapter 3 discusses discontinued operations.

Financing activities

Note in the annual statement of cash flows for the business example (refer to Figure 5-1 or 5-2) that cash flow from operating activities is a positive $1,515,000 and the negative cash flow from investing activities is $1,275,000. The result to this point, therefore, is a net cash increase of $240,000, which would have increased the company's cash balance this much if the business had no financing activities during the year. However, the business increased its short-term and long-term debt during the year, its owners invested additional money in the business, and it distributed some of its profit to shareholders. The third section of the cash flow statement summarizes the *financing activities* over the period.

The managers did not have to go outside the business for the $1,515,000 cash increase generated from its operating activities for the year. Cash flow from operating activities is an *internal* source of money generated by the business itself, in contrast to *external* money that the business raises from lenders and owners. A business does not have to go hat in hand for external money when its internal cash flow is sufficient to provide for its growth. Making profit is the cash flow spigot that should always be turned on.

A business that earns a profit could, nevertheless, have a *negative* cash flow from operating activities — meaning that despite posting a net income for the period, the changes in the company's assets and liabilities cause its cash balance to decrease. In reverse, a business could report a bottom-line *loss* for the year, yet it could have a *positive* cash flow from its operating activities. The cash recovery from depreciation plus the cash benefits from decreases in its accounts receivable and inventory could be more than the amount of loss. More realistically, a loss usually leads to negative cash flow, or little positive cash flow.

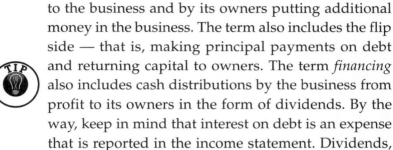

The term *financing* refers to a business raising capital from debt and equity sources — by borrowing money from banks and other sources willing to loan money to the business and by its owners putting additional money in the business. The term also includes the flip side — that is, making principal payments on debt and returning capital to owners. The term *financing* also includes cash distributions by the business from profit to its owners in the form of dividends. By the way, keep in mind that interest on debt is an expense that is reported in the income statement. Dividends, on the other hand, are not expenses reported in the income statement. Dividends are deductions from retained earnings. Chapter 3 discusses the statement of retained earnings.

Most businesses borrow money for the short term (generally defined as less than one year), as well as for longer terms (generally defined as more than one year). In other words, a typical business has both short-term and long-term debt. (Chapter 4 explains that short-term debt is presented in the current liabilities section of the balance sheet.)

The business in the example has both short-term and long-term debt. Although this is not a hard-and-fast rule, most cash flow statements report just the *net* increase or decrease in short-term debt, generally with financial institutions, not the total amounts borrowed and total payments on short-term debt during the period. In contrast, both the total amounts of borrowing from and repayments on long-term debt during the year are generally reported in the statement of cash flows — the numbers are reported gross, instead of net.

In the example, no long-term debt was paid down during the year, but short-term debt was paid off during the year and replaced with new short-term notes payable. However, only the $100,000 net increase is reported in the cash flow statement. The business also increased its long-term debt $150,000 (refer to Figure 5-1 or 5-2).

The financing section of the cash flow statement also reports the flow of cash between the business and its owners (the shareholders of a corporation). Owners can be both a *source* of a business's cash (capital invested by owners) and a *use* of a business's cash (profit distributed to owners). The financing activities section of the cash flow statement reports additional capital raised from its owners, if any, as well as any capital returned to the owners. In the cash flow statement, note that the business issued additional shares for $150,000 during the year, and it paid a total of $750,000 cash dividends from profit to its owners.

Speaking of cash dividends from profit to shareowners, you might note that in the executive summary to the president, the $750,000 cash dividends are deducted directly from the $1,515,000 cash flow from profit for the year, which leaves $765,000 for other business purposes. It makes better sense to "match up" the cash flow from profit (operating activities) and how much of this amount was distributed to the owners. This is a natural comparison to make.

However, the official financial reporting standard for private companies in Canada (ASPE) says that cash distributions from profit should be put in the financing activities section of the statement of cash flows, as you see in Figures 5-1 and 5-2. As for international standards used by public companies (IFRS), dividends paid can be reported as either operating or financing cash flows. For further discussion on this point see the later section "How to Be an Active Reader."

Besides the difference in the treatment of dividends paid when comparing cash flow statements of companies following ASPE and those following IFRS, another potential difference exists. This difference is for the classification of interest and dividends received. For private companies using ASPE, interest and dividends received are revenues and so they increase profit. Consequently, they are included as operating cash flows. For IFRS they can be reported either as operating or investing inflows of cash since they consist of returns on investments. When it comes to interest paid by the business, the distinction between ASPE and IFRS is the same as the earlier description concerning dividends paid. ASPE requires the reporting of interest payments as operating cash flows, while IFRS gives a choice between showing these as financing or operating cash outflows.

The Term "Free Cash Flow"

A term has emerged in the lexicon of finance: free cash flow. *This* piece of language is *not* an officially defined term by any authoritative accounting rule-making body. Furthermore, the term does *not* appear in cash flow statements reported by businesses. Rather, *free cash flow* is street language; the term appears on some finance Internet sites. Securities brokers and investment analysts use the term freely (pun intended). Unfortunately, free cash flow hasn't settled into one universal meaning, although most usages have something to do with cash flow from operating activities.

The term *free cash flow* has been used to mean the following:

• Net income plus depreciation expense, plus any other expense recorded during the period that does not involve the outlay of cash — such as amortization of costs of the intangible assets of a business, and other asset write-downs and impairments that don't require cash outlay

• Cash flow from operating activities as reported in the statement of cash flows, although the very use of a different term (*free cash flow*) suggests a different meaning is intended

- Cash flow from operating activities minus the amount spent on capital expenditures during the year (purchases or construction of property, plant, and equipment)

- Earnings before interest, tax, depreciation, and amortization (EBITDA) — although this definition ignores the cash flow effects of changes in the short-term assets and liabilities directly involved in sales and expenses, and it obviously ignores that most of interest and income tax expenses are paid in cash during the period

You need to be clear about which definition of free cash flow a speaker or writer is using. Unfortunately, you can't always determine what the term means even in context. Be careful out there.

One definition of free cash flow is quite useful: cash flow from operating activities minus capital expenditures for the year. The idea is that a business needs to make capital expenditures to stay in business and thrive. And to make capital expenditures, the business needs cash. Only after paying for its capital expenditures does a business have "free" cash flow that it can use as it likes. In the example in this chapter, the free cash flow according to this definition is the following: $1,515,000 cash flow from operating activities – $1,275,000 capital expenditures = $240,000 free cash flow.

In many cases, cash flow from operating activities falls short of the money needed for capital expenditures. To close the gap, a business has to borrow more money, persuade its owners to invest more money in the business, or dip into its cash reserve. Should a business in this situation distribute any of its profit to owners? After all, it has a cash *deficit* after paying for capital expenditures. But, in fact, many businesses make cash distributions from profit to their owners even when they don't have any free cash flow (as this section just defined it).

How to Be an Active Reader

Your job is to ask questions (at least in your own mind) when reading a financial statement. You should be an active reader, not a ho-hum passive reader, in reading the statement of cash flows. You should mull over certain questions to get full value out of the statement.

The statement of cash flows reveals what financial decisions the business's managers made during the period. Of course, management decisions are always subject to second-guessing and criticizing. And passing judgment based on reading a financial statement isn't totally fair because it doesn't capture the pressures the managers faced during the period. Maybe they made the best possible decisions in the circumstances. Then again, maybe not.

One issue comes to the forefront in reading the company's statement of cash flows. The business in the example (refer to Figure 5-2) distributed $750,000 cash from profit to its owners — a 44 percent *payout ratio* (which equals the $750,000 distribution divided by its $1,690,000 net income). In analyzing whether the payout ratio is too high, too low, or just about right, you need to look at the broader context of the business's sources of and needs for cash.

The company's $1,515,000 cash flow from operating activities is enough to cover the business's $1,275,000 capital expenditures during the year and still leave $240,000 available. The business increased its total debt $250,000. Combined, these two cash sources provided $490,000 to the business. The owners also kicked in another $150,000 during the year, for a grand total of $640,000. Its cash balance did not increase this amount because the business paid out $750,000 dividends from profit to its shareholders. So, its cash balance dropped $110,000.

If you were on the board of directors of this business, you certainly should ask the chief executive why cash dividends to shareowners were not limited to $240,000 to avoid the increase in debt and to avert having shareowners invest additional money in the business. You should probably ask the chief executive to justify the amount of capital expenditures as well.

Would you like to hazard a guess regarding the average number of lines in the cash flow statements of publicly owned corporations? Typically, their cash flow statements have 30 to 40 or more lines of information. So it takes quite a while to read the cash flow statement — more time than the average investor probably has available. Each line of information in a financial statement should be a useful and relevant piece of information. You may question why so many companies overload this financial statement with so much technical information. One could even suspect, with some justification, that many businesses deliberately obscure their statements of cash flows.

About the Authors

John A. Tracy (Boulder, Colorado) is Professor of Accounting, Emeritus, at the University of Colorado in Boulder. Before his 35-year tenure at Boulder, he was on the business faculty for four years at the University of California in Berkeley. Early in his career, he was a staff accountant with Ernst & Young. John is the author of several books on accounting and finance, including *The Fast Forward MBA in Finance, How to Read a Financial Report,* and *Small Business Financial Management Kit For Dummies* with his son, Tage Tracy. John received his BSC degree from Creighton University. He earned his MBA and PhD degrees at the University of Wisconsin in Madison. He is a CPA (inactive) in Colorado.

Cécile Laurin (Ottawa, Ontario) is a Professor of Accounting at Algonquin College of Applied Arts and Technology in Ottawa. She also taught part-time at the University of Ottawa. Her career began in public accounting, performing audits with the firm now known as KPMG. She then became the chief financial officer of three engineering firms, and the international law firm Gowling Lafleur Henderson LLP, now Gowling WLG. She obtained a Bachelor of Administration and a Bachelor of Commerce (Honours) from the University of Ottawa, and is a member of Professional Accountants of

Ontario and Chartered Professional Accountants of Canada. She is the co-author of *Bookkeeping For Canadians For Dummies* and has written several learning tools for professors and students in accounting. Cécile has also developed several distance-learning courses offered through Algonquin College.

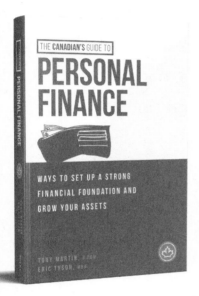
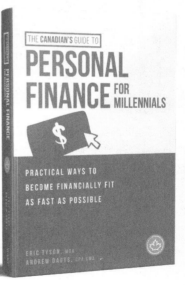

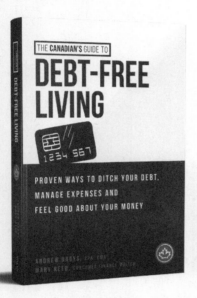

978-1-119-60933-9

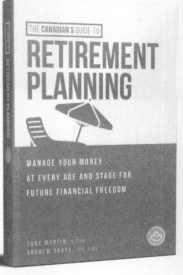

978-1-119-60996-4

THE CANADIAN'S GUIDE TO
STARTING A SMALL BUSINESS

SMART CONSIDERATIONS
AND STRAIGHT FORWARD STEPS TO
LAUNCH YOUR BUSINESS IDEA

ANDREW DAGYS, CPA, CMA
MARGARET KERINS
JOANNE KERTZ

978-1-119-60926-1

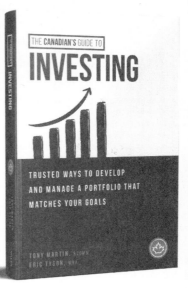

THE CANADIAN'S GUIDE TO
INVESTING

TRUSTED WAYS TO DEVELOP
AND MANAGE A PORTFOLIO THAT
MATCHES YOUR GOALS

TONY MARTIN, BCOMM
ERIC TYSON, MBA

978-1-119-60995-7

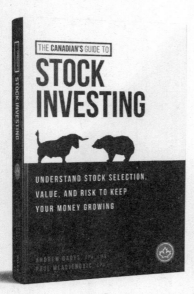

THE **CANADIAN'S** GUIDE TO

STOCK INVESTING

UNDERSTAND STOCK SELECTION,
VALUE, AND RISK TO KEEP
YOUR MONEY GROWING

ANDREW DAGYS, CPA, CMA
PAUL MLADJENOVIC, CFP

978-1-119-61189-9

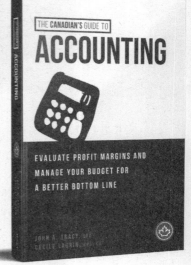

THE **CANADIAN'S** GUIDE TO

ACCOUNTING

EVALUATE PROFIT MARGINS AND
MANAGE YOUR BUDGET FOR
A BETTER BOTTOM LINE

JOHN A. TRACY, CPA
CECILE LAURIN, CPA, CA

978-1-119-60934-6